Tarot: Ethics and Practice

Emma Palmer

2018

Tarot: Ethics and Practice

First Edition: February 2018

ISBN 978-1-908293-47-3

© Emma Palmer 2018

Emma Palmer has asserted her rights under the Copyright, Designs and Patents act 1988 to be identified as the author of this work.

All rights reserved in all media. This book may not be copied, stored, transmitted or reproduced in any format or medium without specific prior permission from the author or publisher.

Published by:

CGW Publishing
B 1502
PO Box 15113
Birmingham
B2 2NJ
United Kingdom

www.cgwpublishing.com

mail@cgwpublishing.com

For more information on Emma and her Tarot services, visit her website, where you can also access the Card of the Day and install a free Daily Tarot smartphone app.

www.emmapsychic.com

Contents

About Me...10

Introduction..12

Your Tarot Deck..15

How to Choose Your Deck..15

Caring for Your Deck...15

The Structure of Tarot..17

Overview..17

The Major Arcana...18

The Fools Journey..19

The Fool (0): Newborn, innocence....................................19

The Magician (I): Conscious mind....................................19

The High Priestess (II): Subconscious mind....................20

The Empress (III): Nurture, mother love.........................20

The Emperor (IV): Authority, father's discipline............21

The Hierophant (V): Education, religion, culture...........21

The Lovers (VI): Love, sex, relationships........................22

The Chariot (VII): Confidence, continued education....22

Strength (VIII): Challenges, endurance, stoicism...........23

Hermit (IX): Solitude, reflection..23

Wheel of Fortune (X): Change, universe, fate.................24

Justice (XI): Fairness, balance..24

Hanged Man (XII): Delay, suspension, giving up..........25

Death (XIII): Endings, rebirth, change............................25

Temperance (XIV): Patience, moderation.......................26

The Devil (XV): Hopelessness, temptation.....................26

The Tower (XVI): Destruction, catastrophe...................27

Star (XVII): Hope, peace, wishes......................................27

Moon (XVIII): Illusion, fantasy, deception....................28

Sun (XIX): Happiness, joy, fun..28

Judgement (XX): Reckoning, assessment.......................29

World (XXI): Completion, wholeness.............................29

The Minor Arcana..30

The Meanings of the Suits..30

Wands...31

Cups..32

Pentacles..33

Swords..34

The Meanings of the Numbers...35

One..35

Two...35

Three..36

Four..36

Five...36

Six...37

Seven..37

Eight...37

Nine..38

Ten..38

Example...39

Court Cards..40

Overview...40

Court Cards In More Detail..42

Complex Personalities...42

The Court Card Ranks..44

Kings..45

Queens...46

Knights..47

Pages..48
Astrology in Tarot..49
Tarot and Astrology Correspondences...............49
Recap on the Elements......................................51
The Meanings of the Planets.............................51
The Meanings of the Signs................................52
Symbolism...53
    Colour Meanings...54
    Symbols..55
    Example..57
Reversals..58
    Example..59
Other Tips to Learning Card Meanings.............60
A Couple of Cards a Day...................................60
Link You Own Experiences................................61
Is There Movement in the Card?.......................61
Use Your Intuition...61
Preparing Yourself for a Reading.......................62
    A Visualisation Meditation...........................62
Reading For Others..65
My Fail-Safe General Spread.............................68
    How I Would Interpret These Cards in a Reading......70
Timing Spread..72
    How I Would Interpret These Cards in a Reading......74
    A Word About Timing..................................76
The Classic Celtic Cross....................................78
    How I Would Interpret These Cards in a Reading......80
The Year Ahead Spread.....................................82

How I Would Interpret These Cards in a Reading..........84
Relationship Spread..........88
　How I Would Interpret These Cards in a Reading..........90
Doubling Up..........93
　Examples of Doubling Up versus Single Cards..........93
The Ethics of Reading for Others..........97
　Be Constructive..........97
　Don't Judge..........98
　No-Go Areas..........98
　The Give-It-To-Me-Straight Types..........99
　Realistic Predictions - Not Wild ones..........99
　Magic Dust..........100
　A Two Way Process..........101
　The Structure of the Reading..........102
Disclaimer..........103

Card Meanings..........105
Major Arcana..........105
　0 - The Fool..........105
　I - The Magician..........105
　II - The High Priestess..........106
　III - The Empress..........106
　IV - The Emperor..........107
　V - The Hierophant..........107
　VI - The Lovers..........108
　VII - The Chariot..........108
　VIII - Strength..........109
　IX - The Hermit..........109
　X - Wheel of Fortune..........109
　XI - Justice..........110

XII - The Hanged Man...110

XIII - Death...110

XIV - Temperance..111

XV - The Devil..111

XVI - The Tower...112

XVII - The Star...112

XVIII - The Moon...113

XIX - The Sun...113

XX - Judgement...114

XXI - The World...114

Minor Arcana...115

Wands..115

   Ace of Wands..115

   Two of Wands...115

   Three of Wands...115

   Four of Wands...116

   Five of Wands..116

   Six of Wands...117

   Seven of Wands...117

   Eight of Wands..117

   Nine of Wands...118

   Ten of Wands...118

   Page of Wands...118

   Knight of Wands...119

   Queen of Wands..119

   King of Wands..119

Cups...120

   Ace of Cups...120

   Two of Cups..120

Three of Cups...120
Four of Cups..121
Five of Cups...121
Six of Cups..121
Seven of Cups..122
Eight of Cups...122
Nine of Cups...123
Ten of Cups...123
Page of Cups...123
Knight of Cups...124
Queen of Cups...124
King of Cups...124
Pentacles...125
Ace of Pentacles..125
Two of Pentacles...125
Three of Pentacles...125
Four of Pentacles...126
Five of Pentacles...126
Six of Pentacles...126
Seven of Pentacles...127
Eight of Pentacles..127
Nine of Pentacles..127
Ten of Pentacles..128
Page of Pentacles...128
Knight of Pentacles..128
Queen of Pentacles..129
King of Pentacles...129
Swords..130
Ace of Swords...130

Two of Swords..130
Three of Swords..130
Four of Swords..131
Five of Swords...131
Six of Swords...131
Seven of Swords..132
Eight of Swords...132
Nine of Swords..132
Ten of Swords..133
Page of Swords..133
Knight of Swords...133
Queen of Swords..134
King of Swords...134

Exercises...135
1: Major Arcana Meanings..136
2: Major Arcana Meanings - Reversals...........................138
3: Minor Arcana - Numbers and Suits............................140
4: Minor Arcana - Numbers and Suits - Reversals.........142
5: Court Cards - Elements and Suits..............................144
6: Court Cards - Elements and Suits - Reversals...........146

Card Reference Guide...148
Major Arcana..148
Minor Arcana...152
Suits..152
Numbers...152

ABOUT ME

As with all things in life, nothing comes easily. My skills with Tarot cards are simply two things I have which anyone can acquire:

- A passionate interest
- The persistence to learn them

Many people have (rather flatteringly said) that I have a "gift" or that I must be super psychic and therefore they could never do what I do. I don't agree. If you are committed to learning the Tarot then you will and nothing can substitute practice. You wouldn't expect to play the piano to a high standard unless you practised it over and over and so it is with Tarot.

I bought my first set of Tarot Cards, Tarot de Marseilles, at the age of 14. I found them in a joke shop which about sums up attitudes towards Tarot in the 1970s. I didn't really know how to read them then and, for a first pack, they weren't the most user friendly. Attitudes have certainly changed since then.

When I was 20 I bought my second set with a basic interpretation book. These are the cards I still use over 30 years later in all my readings; they have lasted me well and I am enormously attached to them. However, I have acquired other sets since then and mostly I would suggest that a new student of the Tarot might like to start with the most classic of decks, The Rider Waite. For the purpose of this book I have used my own Tarot Card designs throughout and my deck is called the Mystic Hare Tarot.

At first I read the cards for myself and then for my friends. I recall that during my twenties and whilst flat sharing, my flatmate would regularly return in the early hours of the morning with her friends and drag me out of bed to do readings for them. I didn't charge for this 24 hour on-call service, but I did receive two beautiful ceramic bowls from a grateful questioner which I still have today.

However, as time moved on, I raised a family and juggled this with a busy career which meant for many years Tarot took a back seat - but it always there like an unseen friend watching my life ready to re-enter at any time. Once my children were grown and many changes had occurred in my life, I no longer took any interest in my career in finance, in fact, I grew to detest it. So Tarot swept back into my life and I haven't looked back.

I have always found reading for myself next to impossible and also for my close friends and family as I am unable to be objective enough. I know too much about my own life and theirs and this will always sway the interpretations and not necessarily correctly. Thus, reading for strangers is far easier as I have no preconceived ideas about their lives and have to rely on my intuition.

So I have realised with all this experience that this is a subject I could teach others so that they also can enjoy an income from Tarot. It is the most simple of businesses - there is no cost of stock (apart from your cards) and the equipment is extremely portable!

I have learned over the years that Tarot is not just fortune telling, but amounts almost to counselling. For the happiest of people never really feel the need to consult a reader about their future, only those who have problems or who are unhappy. I have also learned the importance of empathy and responsibility in reading for people who will often tell you their deepest secrets. These subjects I will cover later on.

In the meantime, if you have any queries about any of the material I have produced here, please do not hesitate to contact me at **readings@emmapsychic.com**

Introduction

Whenever I have a new client in front of me for a reading, I will always ask if they have had a Tarot read for them before. If not, I will always ask if they are aware that there are some scary looking cards in the pack, such as Death or the Devil. It is important to stress at the beginning of a reading that the Tarot Cards are symbolic and not literal. A fellow reader once had a client turn over the table and run out of her shop when the Death card was placed in front of him. What a pity, for Death means the end of *a period* in one's life, NOT the end of one's life. It means change, and I see it as a really positive card!

It is so important to try to deal with myths and misconceptions at the outset, not only of readings but those held by newcomers to reading the Tarot.

Reading Tarot Cards is often made unnecessarily complicated and presented as the preserve of mystics and psychics by unscrupulous practitioners as though they possess some special powers that you do not! Indeed even the media plays up to this misconception. For this reason, it can be very daunting for a newcomer to the cards who may ask themselves whether they have enough psychic ability to read Tarot.

You do not need to be "a psychic" to read the cards - anyone can do it. I believe that in reading the cards a person is, in fact, using their psychic ability or intuition; it just may not feel like they are. People often think that to be a psychic you have a blinding flash of insight or vivid images start to conjure up; in my experience it isn't really like that. The secret is to let impressions and words come to mind and not be afraid to speak these impressions. But this is about confidence and confidence only builds with practice. For this is the centre of using one's intuition and ultimately will turn a standard reading into a meaningful one.

You may well already know that there are 78 cards in a Tarot deck and that if these cards are placed down they might be in the reversed position (i.e. upside down) which means that there are a possible 156 meanings to learn in the deck. This can sound very intimidating and I would say that learning the cards by rote has its place; to a certain extent it does have to be done. But I hope that the following material breaks down a possible 156 meanings into manageable chunks and lays strategies in place for interpreting the cards without necessarily knowing the traditional meaning. For example the card of the Seven of Swords has quite a complex meaning, but even if you do not remember the standard interpretation, if you can remember what Sevens mean and what Swords represent, you arrive at a meaning.

Not a great deal is known about the beginnings of Tarot and there are differing opinions as to their origin. We know that playing cards, upon which modern Tarot cards are based, were used in 15th Century Europe and these had come over from Islamic societies before that.

It seems that Tarot cards first evolved as a game in 15th Century Italy called "Triumph" which included 22 trump cards we now call the Major Arcana in addition to the standard playing cards we would recognise now. The game of Triumph began to be referred to as "Tarocchi" around 1530 and spread throughout Europe. It wasn't until the late 1700s that in France and England Tarot cards, as they were now known, started to be used for divination purposes by believers in the occult.

The most famous Tarot deck has to be the Rider Waite published in 1909 which is packed with symbolism. It is an excellent deck for both beginners and experienced readers alike. Many, many Tarot decks which have been designed since then which heavily reference the Rider Waite in their artwork. For example; Morgan Greer, Robin Wood, Hanson Roberts, Hudes, and Aquarian decks.

However, I am using examples of my own artwork for Tarot cards. The Major Arcana (which I will come on to later) are all animals and they have been chosen because they each carry a quality which I feel is reflected in the meaning of the card.

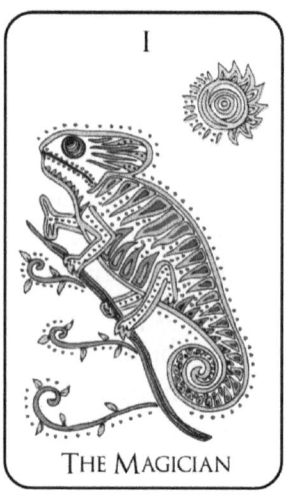
THE MAGICIAN

For example, the Magician is shown as a chameleon. Like the Magician, the chameleon is able to change, transform and adapt to his surroundings. He is able to control his colour to blend in, just as the Magician is able to control his situation.

At the end of this book are a number of worksheets with tasks for you to complete. I know it would be tempting to skip this part (because it's hard work) but I believe that application of the knowledge you have learned via pen on paper is by far the fastest way to get what is rather a large subject in your head. Anyone who has studied for exams will understand this concept. Naturally, there are basic meanings to the cards which are generally understood in the world of Tarot, but we can fashion our own meanings of the cards. This is always the best to use in your future readings as they come from your mind, your psyche and the quality of your interpretations will improve when you trust your intuition. The worksheets are designed to get you thinking and applying your own meanings. If you simply trot out the standard meanings for the cards in a reading, it might be rather wooden and unconvincing. Allow your mind to receive meanings even if they seem a little "off the wall" - this is your psychic ability being exercised.

Your Tarot Deck

How to Choose Your Deck

I have suggested that the Rider Waite is an excellent deck to start with as it is packed with imagery and symbols, but as I mentioned earlier there are many other decks which are based on, or are very similar to, the Rider Waite which you can use. A quick look online will reveal a myriad of different Tarot decks.

I strongly suggest that you choose the deck to which you are most drawn; never mind what anyone else thinks. It might be the artwork, the colours or just a sense of being pulled to them. If you go with your heart on this you will find the deck that jumps out at you or you keep going back to look at, will be the one you work with the easiest. You and your deck will form a bond, just as I have with the Tarot of the Cat People.

You may choose several decks, particularly over the years you may build up a collection but ultimately you will find which one you like best and you will come to love them in time.

Caring for Your Deck

You will need to spend time shuffling, looking at and generally putting your vibrations into your new Tarot deck. There is no substitute for handling them. They need to lose their newness by much handling to begin with. As this is your deck I really would not allow anyone else to play with them. These are not playing cards!

There is much written on the rituals you can perform with your new cards. I prefer to keep it simple. I like to put new cards on a window sill when there is a full moon and allow the moonlight to bathe the cards. This will charge them up. You can do with this crystals to cleanse them also.

You may like to use a smudge stick which is usually made from Sage and pass the cards through the smoke in order to cleanse them of negative vibrations. This is particularly helpful if you have had a difficult reading or felt uncomfortable in any way.

Meditation with your new cards regularly at first will also help you to connect with your deck. You and your deck need time to attune to each other and form a bond.

I wrap my cards in a piece of silk which is intended to keep out negative vibrations. Indeed the silk I use is now as old as my beloved deck; over 30 years and now fraying.

It should be just you who handles the deck but if you are reading for others you need to get them to shuffle it thus lending their vibrations to the cards for the duration of the reading. At the end of reading for someone else you can place a quartz crystal on top of the deck to cleanse it of the their vibrations. Some Tarot readers simply hold the deck in one hand and flick the deck hard with the other which symbolises knocking out negative vibrations.

Many readers also keep their cards in a box. I do think it is nice to have something special such as a patterned piece or silk or a decorative wooden box to keep your cards in. You want to treasure them so they reward you in their turn. Learn to love your cards.

The Structure of Tarot

Overview

There are 78 cards in a deck of Tarot. Within this there are 22 Major Arcana and 56 Minor Arcana - the word Arcana simply means secrets or mysteries.

The Major Arcana is sometimes known as trump cards as Tarot used to be played as a card game centuries ago. As a rule of thumb, Majors are felt to be more significant in a reading as they show significant events or the people that shape our lives, whereas the Minor indicate changing or fluid events which are quickly passing.

The Minor Arcana is divided into four suits (Wands, Cups, Pentacles and Swords.) much like modern playing cards (see below) and range from the Ace through to the King in each of the suits. The Ace through to the Ten in Tarot are sometimes referred to as "pip" cards and there are four "court cards" which include a Page (sometimes referred to as a Princess or a Knave), a Knight, a Queen and a King.

A standard playing card deck has 52 cards whereas Tarot has 56 Minor Arcana - the extra four cards being the Page cards.

The *standard* correspondences with the suits are shown below:

Tarot Playing Cards

- Wands - Clubs
- Cups - Hearts
- Pentacles/coins - Diamonds
- Swords - Spades

I used the word "standard" above, as confusingly, different readers have different correspondences. I personally, see Swords as diamonds and Pentacles as spades! It really does depend on your own interpretation and to be honest, it probably doesn't really matter that much unless you decide to read playing cards which some people do.

The Major Arcana

There are 22 Major Arcana cards in the Tarot deck and these always depict figures in one form or another. The Major Arcana is, as the name suggests, of major importance when it appears in readings. If you have a Tarot spread where a large percentage of the cards are Majors, then you can be sure that this is trying to tell us something very significant - that the question presented is of the utmost importance to the questioner. They also each have a Roman numeral attached to them and have a sequence starting with the Fool at 0 and The World at XXI. The order that the cards are given is meant to represent the journey of life, if we think of the Fool as being a newborn baby who yet knows nothing through to The World which is the accumulation of knowledge and experience we have learned throughout our lives and the end of life's journey. This is often referred to as "The Fool's Journey".

The Fool's Journey is actually quite a profound description for all of us on our lives' journeys. It's full of philosophy and I think we can all identify our own experiences with each of the cards. This structure also helps us remember the order and the underlying meanings to the Major Arcana.

The Fools Journey

The Fool (0): Newborn, innocence

The Fool is a card of beginnings. At the start of his journey, the Fool is a newborn - fresh, open and spontaneous. The Fool is, as yet, unaware of the difficulties he will face in life. In most decks the Fool is shown as he is about to step off a cliff into the unknown.

Zero is an unusual number. It rests between positive and negative as we are at birth - yet to make our own good and bad experiences.

The Magician (I): Conscious mind

On setting out, the Fool immediately encounters the Magician and the High Priestess who are opposites of the whole and are the great balancing forces that make up our world. The Magician is the exposed side - that which can be seen. He represents our consciousness.

The High Priestess (II): Subconscious mind

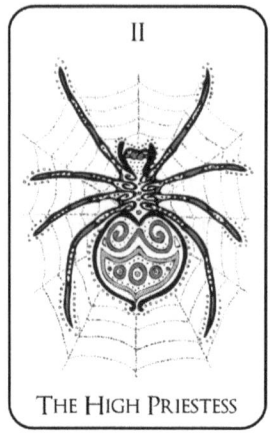

The High Priestess is the hidden side. She is our subconscious and she is our unrealised potential, waiting for our maturity.

The Empress (III): Nurture, mother love

The Empress appears as he starts to grow. The Fool becomes more aware of his surroundings. Most babies first recognise their Mother - the warm, loving woman who nourishes and cares for them. She is the world of love and new sensations. A baby delights in exploring everything he touches, tastes and smells.

The Emperor (IV): Authority, father's discipline

THE EMPEROR

The next person the Fool meets is the Father; the Emperor who is the representative of structure and authority. The Fool discovers order in his world and he also encounters rules. He learns that his will is not always heeded and there are certain disciplines necessary for his own good.

The Hierophant (V): Education, religion, culture

THE HIGH PRIEST

The Fool starts to discover the big wide world. He is exposed to the traditions of his culture and starts his formal education in school. He starts to identify with others and discovers a sense of belonging with new friends. The Hierophant represents organised belief systems such as religion that begin to make an impression on the growing child.

The Lovers (VI): Love, sex, relationships

Eventually, the Fool longs for a relationship with another person and with maturity comes sexual experience. Now he feels the need to fall in love, pictured in the Lovers.

The Chariot (VII): Confidence, continued education

Now the Fool is fully adult and he believes he knows himself with the arrogance of youth.

The Chariot represents the Fool's ego before it has been knocked through experience. The card shows a proud figure riding victoriously, if a little precariously, on his journey. He is in control of himself just for the time being before the road inevitably becomes rough.

Strength (VIII): Challenges, endurance, stoicism

In time, life presents the Fool with challenges; some which cause mental pain and disillusionment. He will need to dig deep and draw on his own Strength. He needs to develop his fortitude, his perseverance and find the heart to keep going despite setbacks.

The Fool also learns that the understated quality of tolerance is not to be underestimated. He realises the forcefulness of the Chariot approach to life should be tempered by kindliness and the power of forgiveness.

Hermit (IX): Solitude, reflection

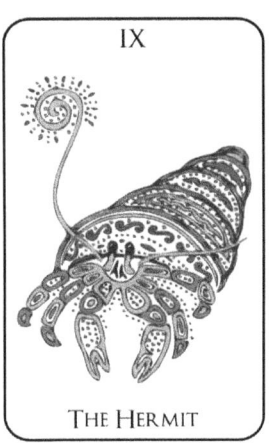

Sooner or later, the Fool may want answers to life's complex questions - what is the purpose of life if in the end we die? Why do others treat us badly? He needs answers which can only be given in the quietness and solitude of reflection, meditation or even spiritual guidance. For the first time in his life, he has a need to be alone.

Wheel of Fortune (X): Change, universe, fate

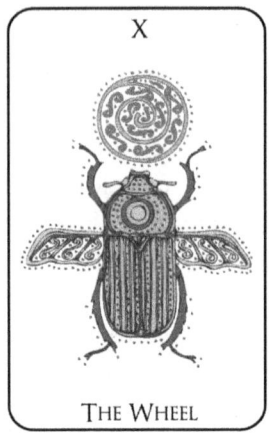

Having been solitary, the Fool now feels ready for action again as he gets an understanding of how everything connects to everything else. His sense of purpose is restored. The Wheel of Fortune is a symbol of the mysteries of the universe which can bring unexpected events and even the feeling of fate. Sometimes some occurrences outside his control can appear almost miraculous - and some disastrous.

Justice (XI): Fairness, balance

The Fool must now take responsibility for his past actions and must pay the price. He may need a dose of rough justice in order to see the consequences of the hurt he has caused others and the poor choices he has made. The demands of justice must be made so that he can move forward honestly. Our Fool needs to choose between an honest route in life or taking the easy dissolute one.

Hanged Man (XII): Delay, suspension, giving up

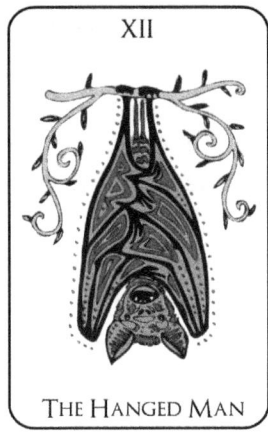

THE HANGED MAN

Full of vigour for his new and honest life, the Fool moves forward believing that life will treat him fairly if he is fair. But he finds life is not so easy to navigate. Sooner or later, he encounters a stumbling block which forces him to give up on a situation and let go. After he has arrived at the giving up point, life starts to move again and the problem is resolved in a way which he could never have envisaged. He learns to place his fate in the hands of the cosmos. The Hanged Man card shows a man suspended by his foot - his world is turned upside down but he is yet calm and at peace.

Death (XIII): Endings, rebirth, change

DEATH

The Fool now begins to eliminate that which he no longer needs in life - either by choice or that which is forced upon him. He goes through a series of endings as he puts the past behind him. This process can seem like dying because it is the death of the familiar which ultimately gives way to the new. At times these changes can be very hard to bear, but it doesn't last forever and is simply a painful rebirth to a new, more fulfilling way of life.

The Structure of Tarot

Temperance (XIV): Patience, moderation

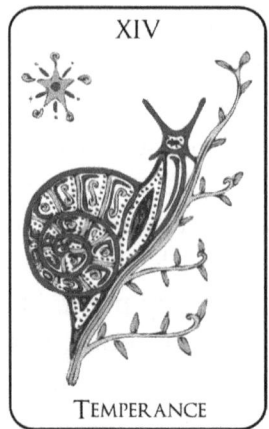

Since the Hermit, the Fool has been on an emotional roller-coaster. Now, he comes to feel the stability offered by Temperance as he recovers his equilibrium. He knows it is acceptable to have to wait for the good things in life. By experiencing the extremes, he has come to appreciate moderation. The Fool has come a long way in realising the joys of a harmonious life.

The Devil (XV): Hopelessness, temptation

Just when the Fool has found peace of mind and a healthy attitude to life, just when he thought he'd experienced it all then life throws another problem his way. He soon comes face to face with the Devil and all that he encapsulates.

This is the devil within us which leads us to hopelessness, despair, addictive tendencies and enslavement to people or material things. The acquisition of material goods can become all consuming so we forget our spiritual side needs nourishment.

The Tower (XVI): Destruction, catastrophe

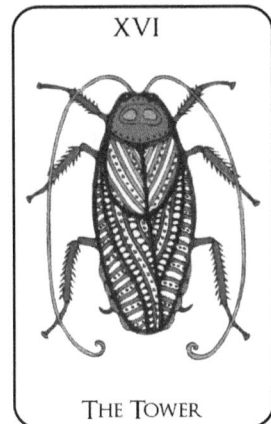
THE TOWER

How can the Fool free himself from the enslavement of the Devil? The release is found through sudden and often devastating change represented by the Tower. The Tower is the hard, ego fortress each of us has built around our pure inner core. It is the prison we create for ourselves.

It sometimes takes a huge crisis to smash through these cold, hard walls of the Tower we build around us - the card traditionally depicts a lightning bolt hitting the Tower. Although such an event can seem like a calamity, it creates a revelatory experience and the soul is then free to carry on in purity and away from despair.

Star (XVII): Hope, peace, wishes

THE STAR

The Fool emerges from the Tower's nightmare scenario into a beautiful period of peace and hope. Traditionally the woman pictured on the Star card is naked as her soul and purity need no disguise. The Star card is a beacon of light, hope and good fortune.

The Fool can start to trust again that life will become wholesome and good. His faith in himself and the future is restored. He is free to know real hope, joy and to make a wish.

Moon (XVIII): Illusion, fantasy, deception

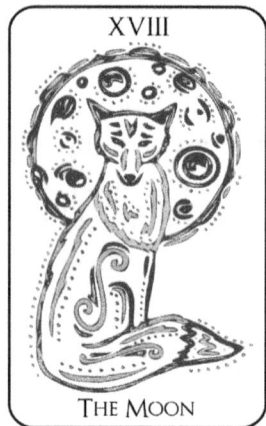
THE MOON

But after this respite there is always another lesson in life to learn no matter how old we are. The Fool has relaxed and now is vulnerable to the illusions and delusions of the Moon. He has relaxed his guard and in his dreamy state of mind, the Fool is prone to fantasy, deceit and trickery. Self deception is very powerful and can create beautiful fantasies which mask the ever present fears lurking beneath.

Sun (XIX): Happiness, joy, fun

THE SUN

Now the Sun has come to illuminate and shine on all our hidden places. Clouds of fear and doubt are gone. Now our Fool is free to enjoy renewed energy and optimism for life. He feels happiness and very blessed. The Sun traditionally depicts - apart from the Sun itself - a baby or young child. Even in our later years we can still retain a youthful joy and enthusiasm for life.

Judgement (XX): Reckoning, assessment

The Fool is nearing the end of his journey and can look back and think about all that he has discovered, good and bad about life. His ego has been shed, his love of material things has a sense of proportion and he allows himself to revel in the simple pleasures of life. He has at last discovered his true vocation. He has discovered how to be happy, truly content. He is absolved and ready to start the final phase of his journey.

World (XXI): Completion, wholeness

The Fool sees the World as it really is but with a more complete understanding than at the beginning. He has integrated all that he has learned and put together all the different aspects of himself - he has become whole. The Fool has had many varied experiences and his accomplishments are many. He has survived this life and all its trials - he has succeeded.

The Fool's Journey shows him to be no fool at all.

The Minor Arcana

There are 56 Minor Arcana cards in a standard Tarot deck and they are numbered from One (known as the Ace) through to Ten, then there are four court cards - more of these later. Minor Arcana may not have the power or significance of the Major Arcana but they are of course very important in telling the story and adding colour and detail to readings. They tend to show events which are temporary and quickly passing out of the questioner's life. A list of the meanings of these cards is shown later on.

The Meanings of the Suits

Suit	Upright	Reversed
Wands	Action, Ideas, Work	Delusion, Egotism, Recklessness
Cups	Love, Emotion, Family	Cold, Unrealistic, Over Emotional
Pentacles	Money, Assets, Materialism	Materialistic, Mean, Greedy
Swords	Ambition, Courage, Power	Anger, Abuse, Conflict

Wands

- Primal energy
- Determination and strength
- Creativity and original thought
- Ambition
- Expansion

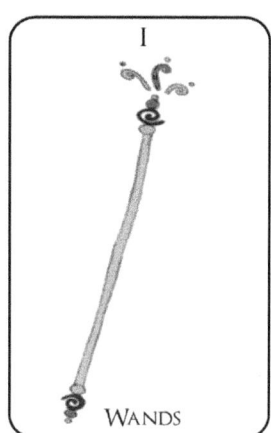

Wands show us what is important at the core of our being. They address what motivates us within our egos, our interests and our self-perception.

Wands are also indicative of all our everyday activities, say working in the office, being at home or being outside in nature. Wands are all about movement, action and the birth of projects. They can be indicative of a person who has many initiatives on the go keeping them busy.

The negative aspects of Wands (i.e. usually when Wands are reversed - see item on reversals) include delusion, egotism, recklessness, a lack of purpose, or feeling a lack of direction.

When referring to timing in a Tarot reading, the Suit of Wands traditionally represents Spring or weeks. Thus in a timing question (rather than the meaning) the five of Wands may indicate an event five weeks from the reading.

Should a Tarot reading be predominantly Wands cards, then you can be sure that the questioner is seeking solutions to issues mainly to do with career or life's purpose. The questioner may also be seeking greater meaning to their lives and although this is often regarding career it can be of a spiritual nature too.

Cups

- Love, marriage and partnerships
- Feelings, displays of emotion
- Family and friendships
- Caring
- Creativity, fantasy and imagination

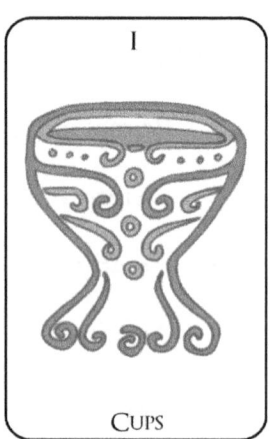

Cups rule our emotional, humanitarian and creative nature. They are about our families and other relationships, and, above all our feelings rather than thoughts or actions. Cups represent how we feel about the world around us and how we connect on a spiritual level to others

The negative aspects of Cups (i.e. usually when the Cups cards appear reversed) include being overly emotional or disinterested and lacking compassion. This can also mean when love is fading and also living in fantasy land - being totally unrealistic. There may be repressed emotion and an inability to communicate properly. Suppression of creativity can cause spiritual unease.

In terms of timing, the Suit of Cups traditionally represents the Summer or a period of days (but usually only if the Cups card is next to a Pentacle card).

The people represented by Cups (i.e. typically the Court Cards) are emotional, artistic, humane and creative. They will probably love animals and nature and be very affected by suffering in others.

In a reading which is dominated by Cups you can be sure that emotions are running very high in the questioner's life, this will be a reading dealing with love, relationships of all form and extremes of feelings.

Pentacles

- Work and business
- Commerce
- Property and other assets
- Practicality
- Money and prosperity

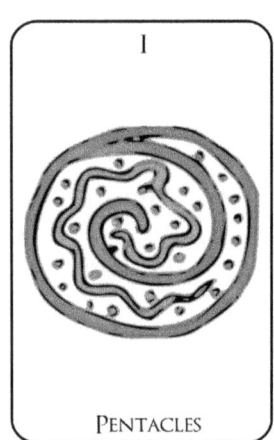

Pentacles deal with the physical or external side of our existence and thus reflect the outer manifestations of our career, finances and productivity. They have to do with what we make of our lives through our environment - how we create, shape and grow it. This is very much about that which is tangible rather than cerebral.

The negative aspects of Pentacles (i.e. usually when Pentacles appear reversed) include being acquisitive, greedy and materialistic - where the love of money starts to corrupt a soul. Over-indulgence and neglect of one's health is also indicated in the negative position. Being reckless and squandering money - even gambling. Or to be overly focused on career to the detriment of family and loved ones.

In terms of timing, the Suit of Pentacles traditionally represents the Autumn or a period of years, however I feel that an indication of months is often more realistic..

Pentacles people are practical, career driven and financially capable. They are often sensual and seek out pleasurable, indulgent experiences.

Should a Tarot reading be predominantly Pentacles cards, then the questioner is seeking answers to material matters, financial concerns and their career.

Swords

- Action, change and power
- Ambition and courage
- Thoughts and inspiration
- Oppression and danger
- Conflict and battles

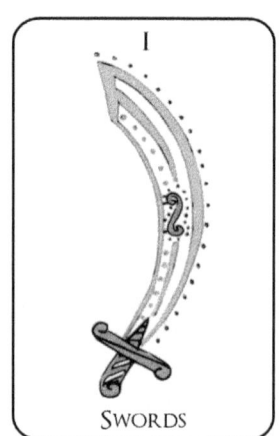

SWORDS

The Suit of Swords is concerned with mental activity and the intellect in addition to the meanings above. Swords show the state of your mind by your thoughts, attitudes, and beliefs. Swords in themselves are double-edged and thus the suit symbolises the balance between intellect and power and how these factors can be used for wrong doing.

The negative aspects of the Suit of Swords (i.e. usually when Swords appear reversed) include anger, abuse both physical and mental, a lack of compassion and generally difficult times.

When referring to timing in a Tarot reading, the Suit of Swords represents Winter or months.

On a positive note, Swords people are intelligent, logical and have excellent communication skills. They are rational and like to experience the world by analysis. On the other hand, Swords people can be ruthless, tyrannical domineering, confrontational and sometimes cruel.

Should a Tarot reading be mostly Swords cards, then you can be sure that the questioner is wanting answers to mental struggles, conflict, arguments and how to make important decisions. Swords can carry negative or very strong messages, however, they also should be taken as a warning to tread more cautiously and take notice of what is occurring around you.

The Meanings of the Numbers

As I have gained in experience of Tarot, I find I increasingly refer to the numbers in the Minor Arcana as a way of adding meaning and depth in a reading. I have indicated below what the numbers of One through to Ten mean in the Tarot. This is particularly relevant in the Minor Arcana and to a certain extent the Major as well. If you want to know what any of the Major Arcana cards equate to then simply consider that these numbers represent a cycle within a cycle, so after card number ten, the cycle starts again. Justice (11) equates to 1, The Hanged Man (12) equates to 2, and so on. Finally, The World (21) brings us back to 1.

One

Number Ones are known as Ace cards in Tarot. The number One shows new beginnings or something in its initial stages. Aces can mean ideas yet to be put into practice - the planning stage so to speak. More than one Aces in a reading indicate that there is something new in the questioner's life or just coming together. Ones are new opportunities or positive changes. They are about potential, ideas, drive and inspiration.

Two

In Tarot, Twos are about choices, decisions, balance and duality. We all come to a fork in the road at times in our lives and this necessitates having to choose a direction. This is about an area where we do have control and the decision being faced is very important. This message is particularly strong where several Twos in a spread appear as it indicates a complex or difficult choice and also a lack of confidence in making that decision. Relief is usually found once the decision is made.

Three

Threes are the culmination of Ones; beginnings, and Twos; choices, and are the end of phase One in a larger cycle. Threes often come up where there are group dynamics at work - often several people are involved in influencing circumstances. When there are several Threes in a reading, it talks of friendships, communication, goals and creativity. It also means group activities. On a less positive note, multiple Threes can mean disorganisation and too many others getting involved. It can mean misunderstandings and even chaos. Multiple Threes means the questioner needs to take charge and not be led by others.

Four

The number Four shows the process of manifestation where projects already started in the first three numbers are starting to grow into fruition. Fours are about stability and putting down roots. They are about structure, foundations and often refer to property. Many Fours in a reading show manifestation from hard work put in before this stage and the potential for growth and addition. In a negative light, many Fours show disappointment that things are not exciting or moving fast enough. Perhaps there are delays.

Five

Fives are about the lack of control and instability. These cards are all about conflict, loss, sadness, anger, challenge and stress. Where there are more than one Five you can be sure the questioner is going through some pretty tough times and emotional difficulty. These cards show a need for spirituality and intuition in order to help them overcome their problems rather than using logic which is no help here.

Six

Sixes are about the self, harmony, family, balance and compassion. They show the way to self resolved solutions for the conflict of Fives. Sixes are a time of adjustment, overcoming problems and self empowerment. These numbers show a time for reflection and maturity. More than one Six adds further emphasis to resolving conflict and creating solutions. Several Sixes are about the home and family if upright it shows comfort, love and care. If reversed there may well be several problems connected to family relationships.

Seven

Sevens are the number of introspection and intuition. In Tarot Sevens come up during periods of solitude or the need for it. These are the cards of assessing our true needs from those we think are our needs. This is the number of spirituality and those things which are hidden. There is also a strong connection to delusion and hopeless fantasy. Several Sevens show the need for reflection, assessment, spirituality and being honest with oneself.

Eight

The Eights in Tarot tend to represent power, energy and positive changes that are taking place. Eights often speak of "spiritual luck" and blessings of abundance that manifest. Eights are about realising our goals. An abundance of Eights in a reading is a sign of personal power, quiet strength and achievement. It shows positive control regained over our lives. There will be a positive change of mind towards a certain situation.

Nine

After the accomplishments of Eights, Nines in Tarot show the feeling of needing to start something new. They also show stability and stasis. When Nines appear more than once it indicates that events are passing our of our lives, but the future direction hasn't been decided so there is a bit of a fluid or a transition period in to come. This often means that Nines leads to feelings of more anxiousness and uncertainty.

Ten

Tens in Tarot mean something has come full circle and the end of a particular cycle in one's life. A new beginning is very much on the horizon. Several Tens can mean difficulty in letting go of the past which may be keeping the questioner stuck in some way. A lot of Tens can mean a time to start to feel hopeful after a difficult cycle, there is rebirth on the horizon and better times ahead.

Example

I recently did a reading for Sandy (not her real name) and she asked me if she would ever find love again. She had been through a very traumatic few years in her love life and in health and felt so low. It seemed as though everyone she met was flaky or not interested. She was a young and attractive lady who really should have no problems in attracting new love.

So for her reading I pulled 15 cards out and to my surprise there were all four Eights and three Tens. This is quite remarkable if you think of the probability of that happening so it was really necessary to take into account the meanings of the numbers. It seemed to me that the Eights showed her moral strength and courage which she has developed through awful adversity and also her feminine power. So although she didn't feel attractive or particularly strong - the Eights revealed otherwise. She has so much more strength than she believes she has and will in time come to see this. Life has been rough but she will feel the benefit of this experience in personal growth. This is a lady who has swum not sunk. The Tens strongly indicate the end of a phase in her life and her being on the cusp of new beginnings; all the difficulties in finding a partner were coming to an end.

So the numbers told me quite a lot without actually reading the meanings or looking at the suits. Tarot reading is not just learning the traditional meanings by rote but by piecing together different considerations such as numbers, the elements, the suits and reversals. More of this later in the Readings chapter.

COURT CARDS

Overview

Court cards are still part of the Minor Arcana and are represented by Kings, Queens, Knights and Pages. In some decks the Knights and Pages are Princes and Princesses respectively. Think of a deck of regular playing cards, the only character missing is the Page.

I have always felt that court cards are, to the novice reader, the most difficult cards to interpret in the whole deck. However, with the benefit of experience, I now find these cards are perhaps the most illuminating about other people's characters and motivations, so it is for that reason I wish to devote some time to this area of the Tarot deck. If you can get a good understanding of the court cards, you'll get the most satisfaction and positive feedback in your readings for being "spot on" about people in the questioner's life.

Court cards represent people in the questioner's life, including the questioner, almost invariably, but confusingly they can very occasionally represent situations. Trying to decide which scenario, a person or a situation, is quite hard to do.

To add to this confusion, Kings are usually men, but they can represent women too! The same is true for the other court cards. Gender is indicated but not assured. I have made the error in the past of referring to the King which appeared in a lady's reading as being her male partner. The King did indeed relate to her partner, but this was a gay relationship, so the King represented her female partner. I also learned never to assume a person's sexuality. You can often think more about the male and female characteristics of the cards, instead of taking them as literally representing a man or woman.

So, you cannot be certain whether a court card is:

- Male or female

- A person, the questioner or a situation

Great! Well, the short answer is you have to look at position of the card and look at other cards surrounding the court card in question and let your intuition guide you.

The other aspect which you may find in other books on interpretation of court cards is a reference to a person's colouring dependent on the suit; for example Cups = blonde, red hair, fair skinned, light complexion. Personally I totally disregard this unnecessary layer of complication because I feel that it does not allow for racial characteristics. If you were reading for a person whose partner was black and represented in a reading by the Queen of Cups, it might make your reading look wrong from the outset to start describing this partner as being blonde with fair skin. Thus I feel that interpretations from the cards on physical traits is outmoded and old fashioned.

Similarly, Tarot cards are often linked to astrological signs e.g. The King of Wands is associated with Aries. If you want to describe a person who has appeared in a reading by stating their star sign, I feel you've got about a one in 12 chance of getting it right! For me it doesn't work. The characteristics of Aries are what is important, it rarely actually represents a person's sign in my experience. I have included in the Astrology section, a chart showing the Major Arcana and their links to planets and astrology - this is for reference and I would reiterate it is the characteristics of say, Pisces, which is a useful tool, not trying to second guess that a person is a Pisces! Personally, I tend to keep astrology out of a reading. Let us not confuse the two subjects, Tarot and Astrology, as they are both vast in their own right.

Court Cards In More Detail

There are four royal families in a Tarot deck - one per suit of Wands, Cups, Pentacles and Swords. To reiterate the overview above, each family has four members - King, Queen, Knight and Page. Thus there are 16 court cards.

Complex Personalities

These 'personality' cards illustrate the whole range of human characteristics - good and bad. It hardly goes without saying that just one card can fully represent an actual person. Humans are all so complex that to squash a human personality into the symbolism of a single Tarot card would be impossible. But a card can reflect *aspects* of a personality or their attitude towards a certain situation.

When learning about the court cards, I feel it helps to take a fairly structured two layered approach. I want to outline a basic framework into which you can start to interpret various personalities.

The first layer to consider:

Each court card is dominated by the qualities of his or her suit - so let's recap briefly:

- Wands represent the element of fire and the realm of action, dynamism and inspiration

- Cups represent the element of water and the realm of family, emotion and intuition

- Pentacles represent the element of earth and the realm of practical matters, such as money, jobs and property

- Swords represent the element of air and the realm of thought, intellect and communication

The second layer to add in:

Each royal rank is also assigned an element. Kings are fire, Queens are water, Knights are air and Pages are earth. This starts to add depth and dimension to the card.

We can assign general personalities to the elements as follows:

Fire: Temperamental, active, inspired, enthusiastic. This personality can burn bright but also experience burn-out - can be exhausting company.

Water: Emotional, feeling, intuitive, expressive. This personality often changes so much that it is difficult to get a grasp on their motivation. Can become depressive individuals.

Air: Intellectual, thinking, logical. Air personalities are good communicators, excelling in the use of words for their cause. They can also use words to wound.

Earth: Practical, matter-of fact. Earth personalities often combine some of the characteristics of the other three but in a down-to-earth, pragmatic way. Can come across as a bit dull. Either excellent or hopeless with money.

See table below for correspondences:

Suit/Rank	King	Queen	Knight	Page
Wands	Fire + Fire	Fire + Water	Fire + Air	Fire + Earth
Cups	Water + Fire	Water + Water	Water + Air	Water + Earth
Pentacles	Earth + Fire	Earth + Water	Earth + Air	Earth + Earth
Swords	Air + Fire	Air + Water	Air + Air	Air + Earth

Court Cards   43

Let's look at two examples.

The King of Swords is a combination of air and fire, with air, as the suit, being dominant. This means that the King of Swords is predominantly a thinker and his secondary characteristic is of action. Therefore, when faced with a challenge he will *act* in accordance with his *logical thoughts* rather than his intuition (which would be King of Cups).

The Queen of Pentacles is practicality (earth) tempered by intuition (water), therefore her *decisions* are made with both feet on the ground with due regard to the *feelings* of others.

With this secondary layer of the four elements you can start to see how this would look in a real person. Of course these characteristics are very simplistic but I hope you can see how it works.

There is a worksheet towards the end of this book which will allow you to write your own interpretations of the court cards. Always ask yourself, does this court card remind me of anyone?

The Court Card Ranks

Although the court cards are assigned genders, this should not be followed slavishly. A woman can fit a King personality, and vice versa. (See the overview) To see this would mean you need to think about the masculine traits a woman may possess and how does this relate to her reading? Or the feminine qualities a man might have - again what is this telling us in his reading? Please do not be tempted to think this is as simplistic as indicating a person's sexuality. It doesn't! I think we are all a mix of both genders in our make up to a greater or lesser extent. The most androgynous court cards are the pages, who can represent children or young people of either sex.

Kings

King	King	King	King
Wands	Cups	Pentacles	Swords

The Kings are considered to be the rulers of their suit in line with stereotypical image of a king being ruler of all. However, this doesn't mean that they are dictators or have reached the height of their achievements, it means that this personality type is masculine, mature, active - in the sense that he prefers taking action to doing nothing. They look outwards and are more interested in events and logic than in people and feelings.

Kings have, or should have, gained clarity and wisdom. In a young person's reading a King would indicate a mature and sensible outlook on life. Like the expression, an old head on young shoulders.

Queens

| QUEEN | QUEEN | QUEEN | QUEEN |
| WANDS | CUPS | PENTACLES | SWORDS |

Queens also have maturity and experience not reflected in the Knights and Pages. A Queen is comfortable with who she is. Queens are quite introspective and are also very interested in other people. Depending upon their suit, they can be nurturing, seductive, conniving or practical.

Queens are more passive than Kings preferring to watch and learn before acting Queens are also mistresses of game-playing; they can be quite capable of manipulation if they see it necessary. As friends they can either be super reliable and faithful or they can be two faced. Similarly as bosses they can be supportive or, at worst, spiteful depending on the situation.

Knights

KNIGHT	KNIGHT	KNIGHT	KNIGHT
WANDS	CUPS	PENTACLES	SWORDS

Knights are usually young people in their twenties or thirties and are actively moving towards maturity. They are often still searching and have not quite defined their life-path. They are bold, intense and sometimes impulsive as they have not yet learned to restrain their reckless youthful tendencies.

Knights can be disappointing and let people down due to thoughtlessness and a certain amount of selfishness. If this appears in an older person's reading then it can either indicate that they still have a great sense of youth, or they look youthful - definitely no pipe and slippers yet! In a negative context it can mean a mature person is being rather immature.

Pages

| Page Wands | Page Cups | Page Pentacles | Page Swords |

The Pages (sometimes labelled Knaves or Princesses) are the youngest and most immature of the Tarot court cards. They often represent children, teens, young adults and people with a very young outlook. These personality types are still in a stage of development. They are coming to terms with their place in the world and their interactions with other people.

Pages are introspective and practical, but these characteristics are defined within the boundary of their suit. Even a mature person can display aspects of Page personality, especially if embarking on a new venture or life experience. It can indicate the overwhelming desire to escape the stresses and strains of adult life and regress into childish pursuits.

Please find a worksheet at the end of this book for you to fill in with your own interpretations of the court cards.

Astrology in Tarot

For many readers, Astrology has a major role in the interpretation of Tarot cards, however, I am only briefly touching on it here for reference.

The 22 Major Arcana are all represented by either; a zodiac sign (12), a planet (7) or an element (4)

All Astrological signs are governed by a planet and the traditional Tarot system uses only the seven sacred planets of the ancients (Sun, Moon, Mercury, Venus, Mars, Jupiter and Saturn) and does not use the outer planets of Uranus, Neptune and Pluto

Tarot and Astrology Correspondences

Major Arcana Card	Element	Planet	Zodiac
The Fool 0	Air		
The Magician I		Mercury	
The High Priestess II		Moon	
The Empress III		Venus	
The Emperor IV			Aries
The Hierophant V			Taurus
The Lovers VI			Gemini
The Chariot VII			Cancer

Strength VIII			Leo
The Hermit IX			Virgo
The Wheel of Fortune X		Jupiter	
Justice XI			Libra
Hanged Man XII	Water		
Death XIII			Scorpio
Temperance XIV			Sagittarius
The Devil XV			Capricorn
The Tower XVI		Mars	
The Star XVII			Aquarius
The Moon XVIII			Pisces
The Sun XIX		Sun	
Judgement XX	Fire		
The World XXI	Earth		

Recap on the Elements

Fire   Actions, self will, control, inspiration, creativity, energy, initiative, goals, activities

Water   Feeling, emotion, love, friendship, family, dreams, desires, social activity, spirituality, intuition

Earth   Sensations, materialism, strength, endurance, growth, reliability, practicality, pragmatism

Air   Thinking and thoughts, expression, spoken and written communication, conflict, strife

The Meanings of the Planets

Sun   Self consciousness, the will

Moon   Emotional side, imagination, instinct

Mercury   Individuality, intellect, communication

Venus   Love, relationships, pleasure, sensuality, prosperity

Mars   Vitality, energy, sexuality, drive, ambition

Jupiter   Expansiveness, growth, energy, good fortune

Saturn   Materiality, restriction, limitation, the unknown

The Meanings of the Signs

Aries	Dynamism, manifestation; energy, growth, potential, birth
Taurus	Stability, security, intractability, expression, permanence
Gemini	Mental expansion, communication, connectivity, duality
Cancer	Sensitivity, emotions, nurturing, tenacity
Leo	Outward expression, courage, confidence, strength, determination
Virgo	Integration, analytical, critical, self improvement
Libra	Balance, practicality, beauty, harmony
Scorpio	Deep emotion, passion, regeneration, renewal, decay
Sagittarius	Expansion, transformation, spirituality, independence
Capricorn	Order, structure, sacrifice, achievement, practicality
Aquarius	Mindfulness, intellect, selflessness, fairness
Pisces	Spirituality, sensitivity, dreams, faith, intuition

Symbolism

Tarot cards from whichever deck you use are always full of symbols and should be looked at very closely to see what additional information they offer up through their designs. The guide below to what colours and symbols mean is based on the seminal Rider Waite deck of Tarot cards. There are many other Tarot decks in existence and a great many of those are based on the Rider Waite and thus the symbols can apply to these decks too.

It should be remembered that, as always, in Tarot your own interpretation is best of all. If you understand the colour blue to mean something other than in my guide, then go with your instinct! You may notice that some of the colours e.g. yellow, has both positive and negative meanings attached. It is up to you as the reader to decide which to use, but I would also qualify this by looking at the quality of the colour. Is it a bright and clear yellow, or is it a murky yellow? When you are learning Tarot take time to examine each card and see what it "says" to you. Notice any thoughts or impressions you get from it. I cannot emphasis enough how important this is in all aspects of Tarot. Be guided by this book, but use it as a starting point to build up your own meanings.

Colour Meanings

Red   Passion, lust, sex, willpower, courage, strength, anger, power, violence.

Pink   Friendships, family, empathy, harmony, affection, romance.

Orange   Energy, bravery, pride, ambition, enthusiasm.

Yellow   Vitality, success, confidence, happiness, sickliness, cowardice.

Green   Fertility, abundance, prosperity, growth, healing, life force, jealousy.

Blue   Tranquillity, honesty, introspection, peace, freedom, sadness.

Purple   Psychic powers, esoteric knowledge, vision, spirituality, egotism.

Brown   Earth connection, being grounded, stability, boredom, stagnation.

Black   Endings, a void, purity, termination, evil, darkness.

White   Purity, the highest of all spiritual colours

Symbols

ANGELS/CHERUBS: A sending from a Divine messenger - pay heed to what they are trying to tell you. The questioner is being assisted on a spiritual level and is receiving angelic help.

ANIMALS: Think about what the animal represents e.g. a dog in Tarot shows fidelity and trust, a bird would mean freedom (unless he is chained), a fish means subconsciousness and extra sensory perception, a lion means nobility and pride.

BABIES/CHILDREN: Youth, innocence and purity are shown here. Also sometime naivety. It can represent young people either in life or spirit. Either way I feel this is more representative than literal.

CASTLES: Often seen in Tarot, they show protection, safety, wealth and the rewards of success. Is there a winding path up to the castle? If so, the questioner's journey to success or safety is long and difficult. Personal goals should be worked at for success is possible. The castle is a stronghold, an almost impenetrable building and is a good metaphor for projects, stability and structure.

CHAINS: Enslavement or being tied to something or someone. Self limitation - the belief we are trapped when the reality may not be so.

CIRCLES/INFINITY: Circles and the Infinity symbol (it appears like an eight on its side) represent eternity or that life is constantly turning and changing. Through good times and bad, nothing lasts forever. Infinity shows the harmony of the conscious and unconscious minds.

CLOUDS: Symbolic of the element of Air and thus is associated with thoughts, logic, intellect and creative thinking.

CROWNS: Wealth, recognition and achievement. Crowns emphasise materialism and can be lacking in spirituality.

FLOWERS: Innocence, youth and potential. Beauty and freshness. Flowers bloom before they transform into fruit.

FRUIT: Symbolic of fertility, growth, abundance and projects coming to fruition.

HANDS: The right hand shows consciousness and has masculine energy. The left hand is of the subconscious mind and feminine energy. Therefore duality.

KEYS: Keys either unlock doors which lead to freedom or enlightenment or they can lock doors meaning imprisonment, secrets and even protection.

LAMPS/LANTERNS: Spiritual enlightenment through meditation and introspection. They represent intellect and the search for truth and virtue.

LIGHTNING: This can mean inspiration or events striking out of the blue. Lightening is hugely powerful and shows on cards where there are sudden intense experiences. Lightening can be dangerous too so shows us when we need to exercise caution.

MOON: The Moon is feminine and shows our subconsciousness - what is it we have overlooked but our subconscious is trying to tell us. The Moon is a force which can control tides and cause temporary insanity. There is always a sense of the hidden, the occult and secrets when it appears.

MOUNTAINS/HILLS: These show the obstacles we need to overcome or climb in order to reach our goals and desired outcomes. The climbing of a mountain is not easy and neither are some of the things we wish to attain but rewards would great. Hills are a lesser version of a mountain and therefore show some of the obstacles we face day to day. Mountains can also point to ideals and cherished beliefs.

PATHS: We find paths that are either straight or winding and thus is our path in life. The journey towards our goals can be straightforward or take twists and turns. On a more esoteric level the path may show our direction towards gaining spirituality.

SCALES: They show justice, fairness and equilibrium. It is time to weigh up one's options and decide the best and most honest way forward. Where is there a need for balance and justice in the questioner's life?

RIVER/STREAM/WATER: Water in any form is always about the unconscious mind, intuition and emotion. Is the stream flowing with ease or is it sluggish? This will indicate the questioner's state of mind and emotional needs.

SUN: A joyous symbol as it is a source of light and heat, life cannot exist without it. It represents radiance, warmth and energy.

Example

The Lovers (Rider Waite) - Symbolism to Consider

- Angel - Purity, love, divinity
- Clouds - Thought and intellect
- Fruit - Things which are coming to fruition
- Nakedness - Nothing hidden or concealed
- Mountain - Mountains have been climbed to reach here
- Red (angel wings) - Passion, vitality
- Trees - growth and abundance
- Snake - wisdom, original sin
- Sun - Beauty, harmony and joy

REVERSALS

I know of some Tarot readers who only interpret the cards when they are in the upright position and if that works for them then that is fine. My preference is to have the cards come out either in an upright position or reversed i.e. upside down.

I mentioned earlier that there are 78 cards in the Tarot deck and therefore 78 meanings to learn. Most new students to Tarot would find having to learn all the reversed card meanings means twice as much work and when you think about it, 156 really is a most daunting number.

Not to worry though, I actually find reversals an easy concept to learn. You might be tempted to think that a reversed card is the opposite of its upright meaning. Not so - it's more like a watered down version of the upright meaning. It also points to potential, things that might occur are far less definite than when the card is upright. I feel that this is when the questioner has the ability to control events and make positive changes but is still hesitating or procrastinating.

Sometimes people want change but they don't want to put the effort in or are frightened of change - this would be where I see reversed cards which point to potential but unlikely to be realised until action is taken.

Example

Lucy hates her job but has been there 15 years. She has applied for other jobs but been rejected a few times and is feeling undecided as to what to do. In her reading she gets in a future position a reversed Ace of Wands. This would indicate to me that the potential for a new job is very real but by no means assured under the present circumstances - she just needs to keep applying and focus on what is needed to obtain a good new position. The length of time she has been with her company is a hindrance as she might hate her job but there's a certain inertia and a defeatist attitude prevailing. Meaning that a new job is still out of reach but by no means impossible. As a reader you might wonder if she subconsciously doesn't actually want to move jobs. It's hard under these circumstances to give the questioner the answer they want which is that a new job will just magic itself up without much effort on her part. Naturally, when people come for readings they want definite answers and not maybes. But I firmly believe we have to a great extent our destiny in our own hands and the cards cannot be specific about future events if a person is unwilling to put in the effort needed for change.

In summary, I believe that reversals are actually fairly easy to interpret. Sometimes they can lessen the effect of a negative card to be a much softer meaning. The Tower reversed would soften the impact of any difficult situations which may arise i.e. no nasty shocks just problems which need to be faced. The Nine of Swords reversed means that an agonising worry being experienced is going to fade and will pass quickly out of a person's life.

I have given meanings for the reversed cards at the end of this book in the Card Meanings chapter. There is also a worksheet at the back of this book for you to complete with your own meanings.

Other Tips to Learning Card Meanings

We've already looked at:

- Suits and elements
- Numbers
- Court Cards
- Astrology
- Symbolism

So what else can we do to learn the meanings easily?

A Couple of Cards a Day

Study closely a couple of cards a day. Look up their meanings first if need be and consider the elemental nature of the card, the numerological association and all the symbols and colours.

I would recommend you keep a journal and write down what you have learnt. It really is the fastest way to get those meanings embedded in your mind.

Then...Test yourself

Link You Own Experiences

Memory experts create image-based story chains. Try making a story chain for each of the Minor Arcana suits even if it sounds crazy.

You can also try personalising the cards e.g. the Eight of Cups means to walk away from something. So recall a time when you wanted to walk away from something. Was it a relationship or a job? Use your own experiences as reference. Link your memory to the card. Write it down.

Is There Movement in the Card?

Look at the movement in the card, what does it say to you? Look at the Knights; in most decks, two seem static, Cups and Pentacles and the other two look dynamic, Wands and Swords

Is water depicted? Is it fast flowing, trickling, still or stagnant? What does that mean to you?

What is the weather like in the card? Stormy or still?

Use Your Intuition

More important than all the other methods put together is your intuition. Your psychic ability. You possess this ability no more or less than the next person. Your skills in picking up on the unspoken is strong. Let it work for you.

Let your mind receive thoughts and impressions and don't be afraid or too self conscious to say what you get

Trust your intuition and I promise it will reward you.

Preparing Yourself for a Reading

In order to get the most out of the cards and open yourself up to using your innate psychic intuition, it is helpful to meditate as often as you can, particularly at the beginning of your journey into Tarot. I also think it is important if you are going to start to read for other people. If you are dashing around doing many chores and perhaps thinking about what to have for dinner, then this is not particularly conducive to giving an insightful reading. You will need to find some peace and what better than a meditation? Yes it might take 20 minutes or so but you will gain other advantages to meditating; namely calmness and stillness in your being as well as opening yourself up to psychic messages. Like a muscle, psychic ability needs to be trained and flexed regularly. Meditation is also a really good mood enhancer, so if you are stressed or down meditation will really help.

This is one of my favourite meditations:

A Visualisation Meditation

You might wish to start by sitting in a comfortable chair as you don't want to be distracted by being uncomfortable, so do ensure you can relax as much as possible which means no crossed legs or folded arms.

Next close your eyes, banish all thoughts so your mind is as blank as possible; I know it's not easy, it takes practice to empty your mind. Start by imagining there is no chair beneath you and that your body is entirely suspended in nothingness. Once you can no longer feel the chair, imagine sending your thoughts up to a higher plane where the Great Source of All Light is (some may think of this as God). Ask that you may receive the light and see it in your mind's eye come pouring down in a shaft of brilliant light, so white you can hardly bear to look at it. Feel it flood your body from your head, where it enters, down to the furthest extremities of your fingers and toes. You may feel hot or cold at this point. I usually see whiteness behind my closed eyes.

Imagine that your every breath in brings in more pure white light and every breath out pushes away the dark grey, black, murky reds and greens of negative thought; in your mind's eye, see the tendrils of unwanted thoughts float out of the window. We all have negative thoughts and these must be left behind during a visualisation meditation exercise. Once you feel your body has been washed of negative energy, you can now feel clean, bright and glowing from within.

Now picture a flower in bud. My favourite to visualise is a peony as they have large, round buds when closed up. When they open they have a profusion of deep red petals. You must chose which ever flower you can visualise best. Watch it open slowly from bud to fully blown and notice every detail you can. See the colours, textures and even smell the scent. Notice any stamens and the very smallest of details such as the tiny veins in the petals. Concentrate on this for as long as you can; if you manage 20 minutes you are doing very well, but even 10 minutes should suffice.

If you have any interfering thoughts or worries on mundane matters such as the shopping or work, just move these thoughts aside again and again to stop your logical mind taking over. You might also acknowledge these as genuine concerns, and use a notepad to write them down, reassuring your conscious mind that you will attend to them at the right time.

If you receive thoughts and impressions, you may take these as messages from your subconscious (some believe it is your higher self telling you answers to your current concerns.) Your subconscious knows the answer to most of your life's problems; it is in there somewhere. These thoughts are not dredged up by the logical mind, but suddenly appear as either images or words. You will come to learn the difference between what is generated by the logical mind and your intuition. You may find you receive a symbol, something you might interpret for yourself, whatever you receive, try to remember and perhaps record it in a journal.

When you are ready, close the flower up to a bud again. This is most important, whilst the flower was open, your psychic senses were fully open, if you do not close down properly, you will find that you are open to negative energies and you may begin to feel drained. In the worst case scenario you may even be open to psychic attack or unpleasant dreams. Then see the flower fold in on itself and close up to a tight bud, even visualise rain falling on it and see the water droplets run off it because it is closed.

Next, give thanks for the light and any information you have received and close down the top of your head through which you received the light. When you are ready, open your eyes. You will probably feel very relaxed and sleepy, serene even. Notice everything which happens to you and write it down. After doing this a few times, you can compare your experiences and watch how proficient you become over the coming weeks.

Reading For Others

When your questioner arrives for a reading, it is always helpful to engage with some small talk before going straight in for the reading. This helps put the potentially nervous client at ease and also creates a feeling of welcomeness and even trust. I often ask if they have ever had a Tarot reading before and if they understand what the process is. I then tell them I will start with a general reading from which several of the questioner's issues may arise. At this point I do not require any information from them. After the general reading is complete, this is then the chance for the questioner to ask any questions and explore any burning issues they have. This is where the two-way process begins. Although many questioners do start to contribute to the general reading.

I would always ask, at this point, what issues the questioner would like to explore or discuss and to try to get them to formulate a question. This way, we can save time and cut to the chase so to speak. If you are unfortunate enough to have the kind of customer who does not want to take part in the reading and only be astounded at your psychic abilities, it can mean a bit of a guessing game and is a waste of their time and money. It is rare for this to happen but it's very hard work because they are inadvertently blocking you from reading them. Mostly people's problems are highly detailed and personal to them so the cards can be a little limited in the small minutiae of modern life. For example, being stalked on social media is a very modern issue and the cards can only be helpful if some of the background to the problem can be given.

When reading for others, or even for oneself, the obvious way to start is with shuffling the cards. I always ask the questioner to shuffle the cards until they feel ready to stop. Some people find it difficult to shuffle because they are not used to handling Tarot cards which are generally larger than ordinary playing cards. If they really cannot shuffle, then I would suggest asking them to cut the pack into seven piles and then gather them up again in any order. You could also invite them to spread the cards out on the table before gathering them back into a single pile.

But let us assume our questioner has shuffled in the conventional way so now ask him or her to cut the pack into three piles and gather them up in any order. They then hand the pack to you and you are ready to begin. Try to ensure that if you are using reversals in your reading and are face to face across a table with your questioner, than when they pass the deck back to you, you should turn the pack around 180 degrees so that you get the right orientation from when they shuffled the deck, so the cards are upright from their point of view.

Many Tarot readers suggest choosing a "Significator card" that is to say, picking out a card which is to represent the person sitting in front of you. But as this was always traditionally done on a person's appearance. I, by that example, would be a Queen of Cups. A mature fair skinned and fair haired woman. But I have to say, I really cannot see the point in doing this; it doesn't add anything to the reading and then you would have to chose a suitable card from the pack. As I mentioned earlier, this does not really allow for different racial characteristics or for those who wish to remain gender neutral. Therefore, my first card is drawn from the top of the shuffled deck and will represent the questioner; more often than not this card shows their personality but it can also show what is predominant in their lives at present.

I find it is generally easier not to look at the spread as a whole initially, I just make a start on the first card and work my way in allowing impressions and thoughts to flow into my mind.

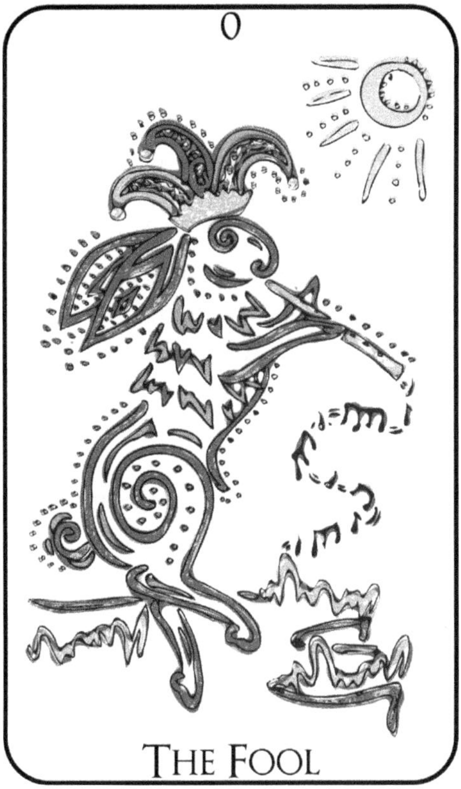
0
THE FOOL

My Fail-Safe General Spread

I nearly always use this spread at the start of a reading as it gives a good overview of the questioner's life at the present. Often all sort of different aspects are thrown up even if they don't look immediately important.

People generally want to hear about the future and whilst the reading will come to this I feel it is always important to look at their past to see what events may have brought them to this point. The past also shows us how a person has dealt with difficult events in life. Position 3 shows difficult or traumatic occurrences in the questioner's life and is important. Say for example, the cards at position 3 show a particularly nasty relationship break up at some point in their history and this same questioner is having problems in creating new and fulfilling relationships now. As a Tarot reader you would be seeing a connection between past events and how they affect the present.

1: The questioner's personality or a significant issue in the present.

2: What crosses the questioner i.e. major issue of concern

3: Events of the distant past - which still have influences today

4: Recent past - from between 12 months ago to yesterday

5: Near future - from between tomorrow and up to 12 months ahead

6: Some more insights into the questioner's attitude and state of mind

7: Outside influences i.e. other people and their effect

8: Likely outcome to present circumstances (another future)

Reading For Others   69

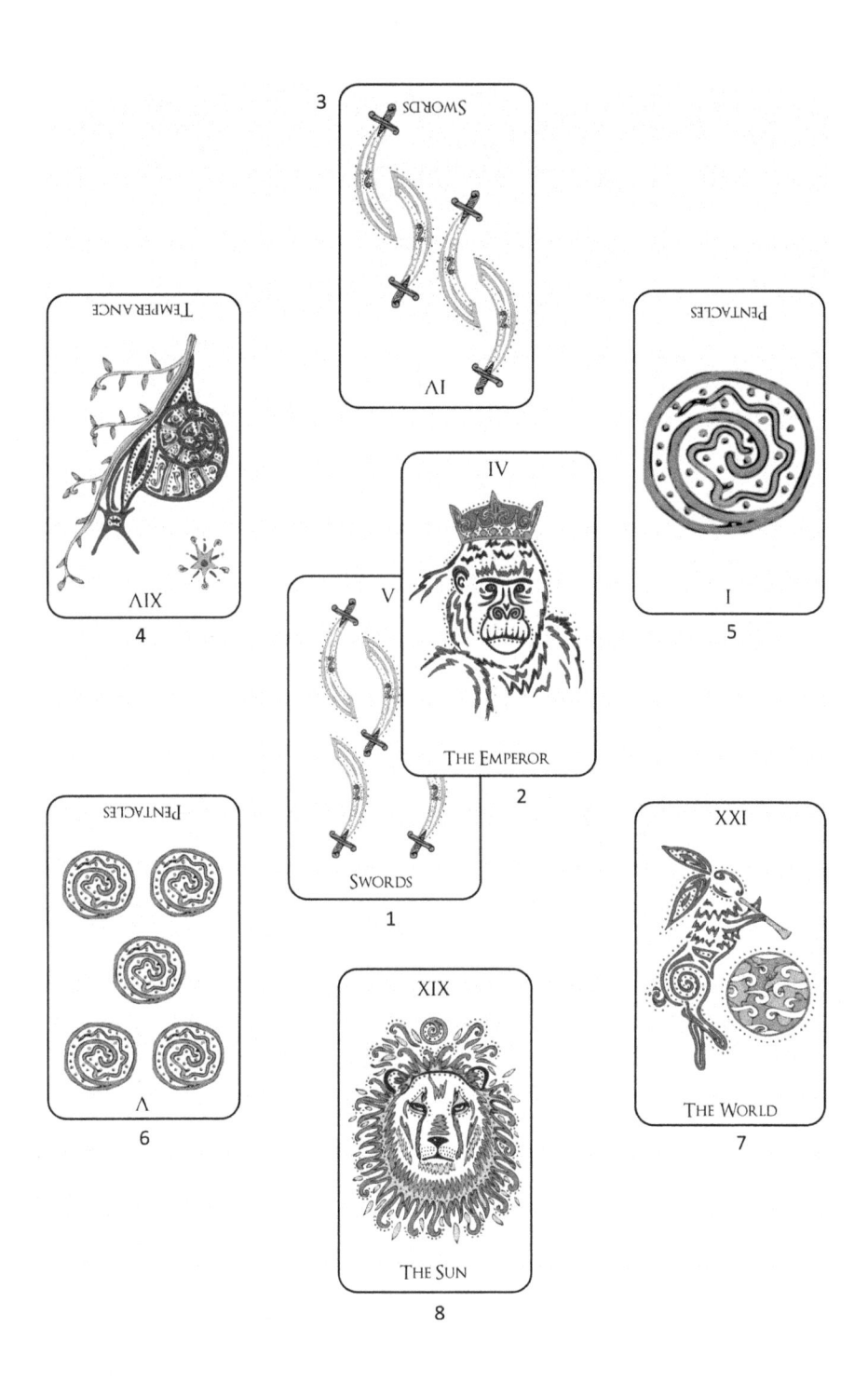

How I Would Interpret These Cards in a Reading

I recently read for Gemma who had these cards come up in her general spread. This spread started to give me a flavour for the issues she has in her life at present and what is most important to her. As it turned out there really was one big concern which dominated this reading.

1: Five of Swords - This would be an issue rather than a personality card as the Five of Swords is about conflict, anger and arguments which are central to her life at present. If she is not having major disagreements with anyone then the conflict may be internal. She is feeling insecure and upset and possibly repressing her anger towards someone.

2: The Emperor shows us the person with whom she is in conflict. The Emperor may be a father figure or her husband. As this was in relation to her husband then we can be sure that the relationship between them is that he takes a dictatorial and overbearing stance in his behaviour towards her and that she allows this - this appeared to be recreating the relationship she had with her father.

3: Four of Swords in the distant past. Gemma has now long since recovered from the difficulties encountered with her father's stern attitude towards her but she has not forgotten this and her present situation is threatening to undermine her peace of mind because she sees her father in her husband.

4: Temperance Reversed in the recent past. Her patience has been sorely tested with her husband. This suggested they have been at odds with each other and she was happy to admit she had lost her temper with him more quickly than she should due to being reminded about her past.

5: Ace of Pentacles Reversed in the near future. There may be issues arising about money and she confirmed this had already been a source of conflict. So for the time being the issues will continue but only in the short term. There is also the potential for Gemma to get a new job or secure a promotion, however, this looks more like a potential than something that will definitely happen. She needs to drive that forward if that is what she wants.

6: Five of Pentacles Reversed in the area of further insights to how the questioner is feeling. Gemma has been feeling very negative and sad about her relationship, almost as though she cannot get through to him and he is shutting her out, she fears the worst. However, as this is reversed it shows a problem quickly passing and the feeling that the worst is over.

7: The World as other people and outside influences. I very much doubted Gemma's husband understood that his behaviour was upsetting her as much as it did. He seemed oblivious and she needed to try a different way to get through to him rather than losing her temper. I also felt he might be planning a surprise holiday for her which would be most beneficial for both of them.

8: The Sun as the outcome. A most joyous and happy card showing that difficulties can and would be overcome. Restored happiness was well on the way and maybe even the possibility of a baby! The message from the cards for Gemma was basically lighten up a bit and try to understand the power of good and clear communication in a non explosive manner. She should not take out her long buried frustrations on her well meaning but occasionally thoughtless husband.

Timing Spread

This is spread is also very useful, not just for timing of events to come but also for shedding light on a particular issue. It focuses on a specific concern a questioner may have rather than looking at their life in general terms.

1: The questioner's personality or a significant issue in the present.

2: What crosses the questioner i.e. major issue of concern

3 & 4: Problems surrounding the questioner, worries, fears or those who cause trouble

5: Near future - from between tomorrow and up to three months ahead

6: Medium term future - between three to nine months ahead (six months average)

7: Longer term future - between nine to 12 months ahead

8: Likely outcome to present circumstances - between 12 to 24 months ahead

Reading For Others   73

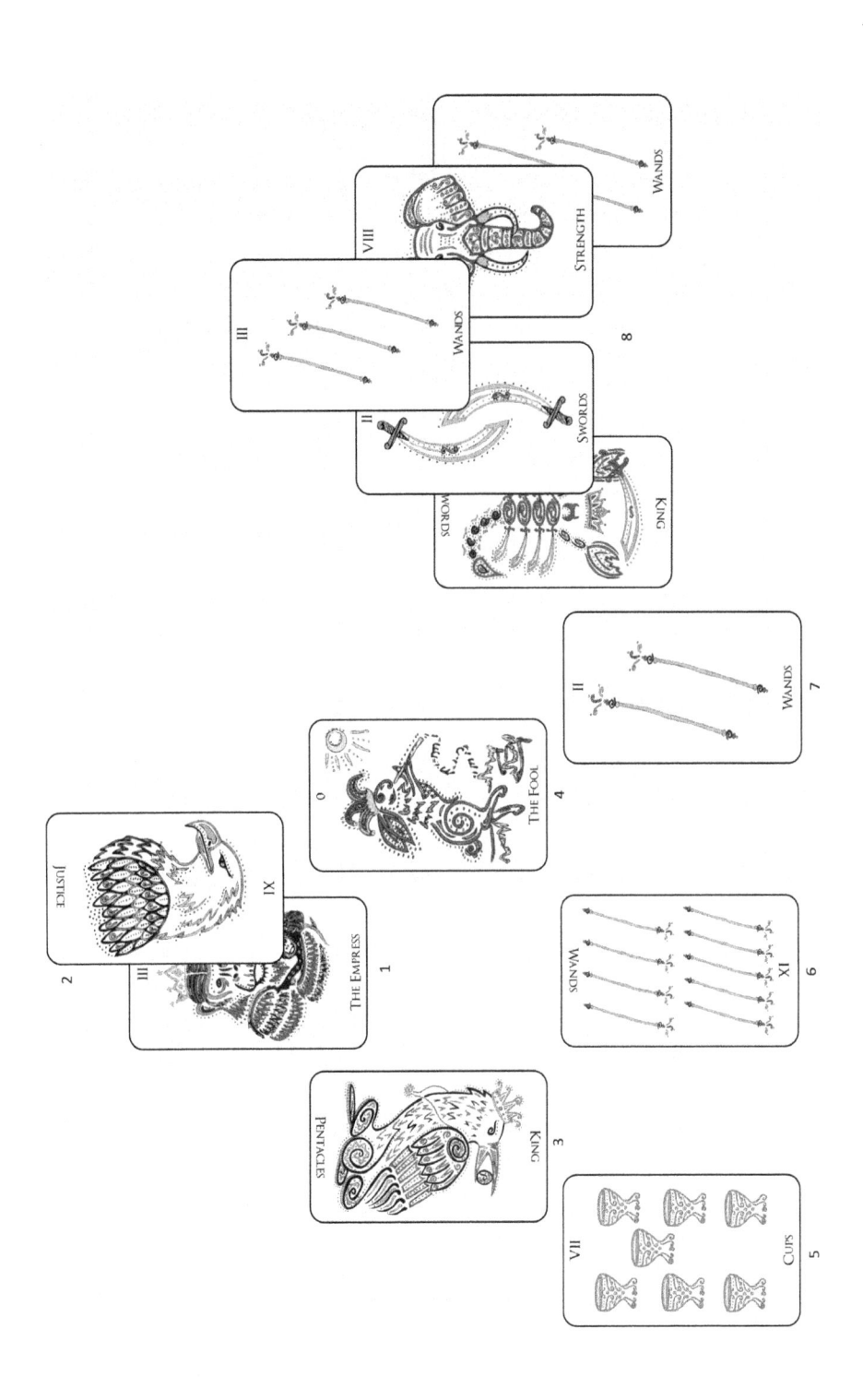

How I Would Interpret These Cards in a Reading

This is a reading I did for Ashleigh a while ago where she really wanted some direction on her career and whether she should stay in her present company or leave to go elsewhere and also should she change her career altogether. She mostly really wanted to know what was likely to happen to her over the next year or two.

1: Empress as a personality card. Ashleigh is caring person who tends to put others before herself and worries what they will think about her. She is a born nurturer.

2: Justice Reversed in the area of what is crossing her. I felt this card had two meanings, firstly it showed me her connections to work in a legal environment (it turned out she was a legal secretary) and secondly as the card was reversed I felt that this line of work was doing her an injustice.

3 & 4: The King of Pentacles Reversed and the Fool represent her fears, worries and the trouble makers in her life. The King immediately tells me she has a difficult boss and particularly so because the card is reversed. He is mean and unlikely to want to pay his staff what they are worth. The Fool showed me she often feels foolish due to being belittled or put down. So I knew that this is not a company that treats its staff with respect. The Fool also points to Ashleigh's desire to step out somewhere new but her confidence is low and she doesn't think she is good enough.

5: Seven of Cups for the near future - the next three months. Ashleigh is still deluding herself she can make a go of it where she is. She doesn't want to admit defeat and thinks if she works hard she will be appreciated but this is fantasy. It is also appears to be easier to remain where she is.

6: Nine of Wands Reversed for medium term future - six months. Under the present circumstances, the pressures are likely to increase for her. She will soon become very burdened by both being lumbered with more work than is fair and also by her unhappiness in her job which is only likely to increase. She needs now to start thinking differently from before. Tried and trusted methods of sticking to her values won't help her here.

7: Two of Wands for longer term future say 12 months ahead. Ashleigh will end up in a bit of a rut unless she acts before she gets to this stage. Inertia won't make the problem go away and she really needs to make a decision to find something new. I feel for longer term happiness she might need to consider a change of direction completely rather than looking for a new job.

8: King of Swords Reversed, Two of Swords, Three of Wands, Strength, Four of Wands as the outcome over the next 12-24 months. Things might get worse before they improve, she may be put under intolerable pressure by her boss (now represented by the King of Swords) and this leads to her being decisive and leaving her job (Two of Swords) and getting a new job with excellent prospects (Three of Wands). The Strength card and the Four of Wands point to her equilibrium and peace being restored from this soul destroying job she has put up with for so long. She will wonder why she didn't do something about it sooner. But hindsight is a wonderful thing. She has to overcome her natural tendency to have a blinkered approach and stick with something even if it makes her unhappy. It's time to try something new.

A Word About Timing

Timing is very important to people and comes up in every reading so it is as well to show how I look at the timing of events. I would also say that as Tarot is not an exact science, if you think a certain event will happen in three weeks time, it might be two weeks or four. Life is not set in stone and events in life can fluctuate depending on our actions and those of others. It's a bit like the weather forecast. Mostly right but subject to some surprises.

If people ask when a certain event will happen and it is not obvious from the spread outlined above, I also use this timing method as well which regards only the numbered Minor Arcana cards (i.e. Ace through to Ten). You should either look at the last card in the spread or work backwards until you see a numbered Minor card and this should be your timing. If you want to confirm this you can also turn a card in response to a direct question for example "when will I meet someone new?". If the first card doesn't help, then keep turning cards until you have a numbered Minor Arcana. Thus the Eight of Swords shows in eight months time, whilst disregarding its usual meaning.

- Wands - Weeks or in the Spring
- Cups - Days (if next to a pentacle) or in the Summer
- Pentacles - Years (or Months) or in the Autumn
- Swords - Months or in the Winter

You can refer also to the notes in The Minor Arcana chapter, in the section The Meanings of the Suits

THE WHEEL

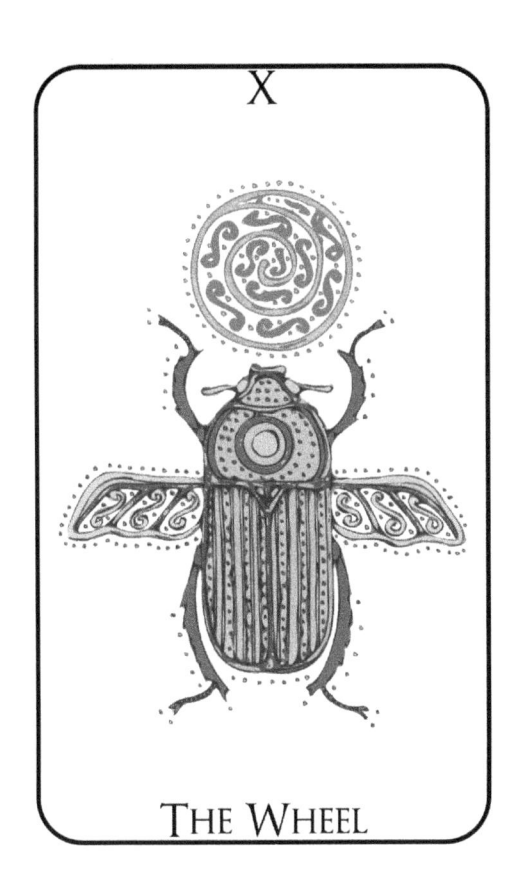

The Classic Celtic Cross

Most Tarot readers use this spread and you will find references to the Celtic Cross spread in any book or website on the subject of Tarot readings. It is not a spread I use very often simply because it takes a little longer due to the volume of cards and I personally like to let my questioners ask as many questions as they like with the employment of the above "Timing Spread". But this is personal choice again and remember, there are no black and white rules in Tarot.

Many readers feel this is a very powerful spread due to its shape and link the Celtic Crosses of Ireland which are often sited on places of great Earth energy.

1: The questioner's personality or a significant issue in the present.

2: What crosses the questioner i.e. major issue of concern

3: Events of the distant past - which still have influences today

4: Recent past - from between 12 months ago to yesterday

5: Near future - from between tomorrow and up to 12 month ahead

6: The best possible outcome to the present situation. The goal or aim.

7: How the questioner affects other people and how he or she is seen by others

8: Other people in the questioner's life and how they affect the questioner's

9: Fears, hopes, worries, sorrows

10: Final outcome

Reading For Others   79

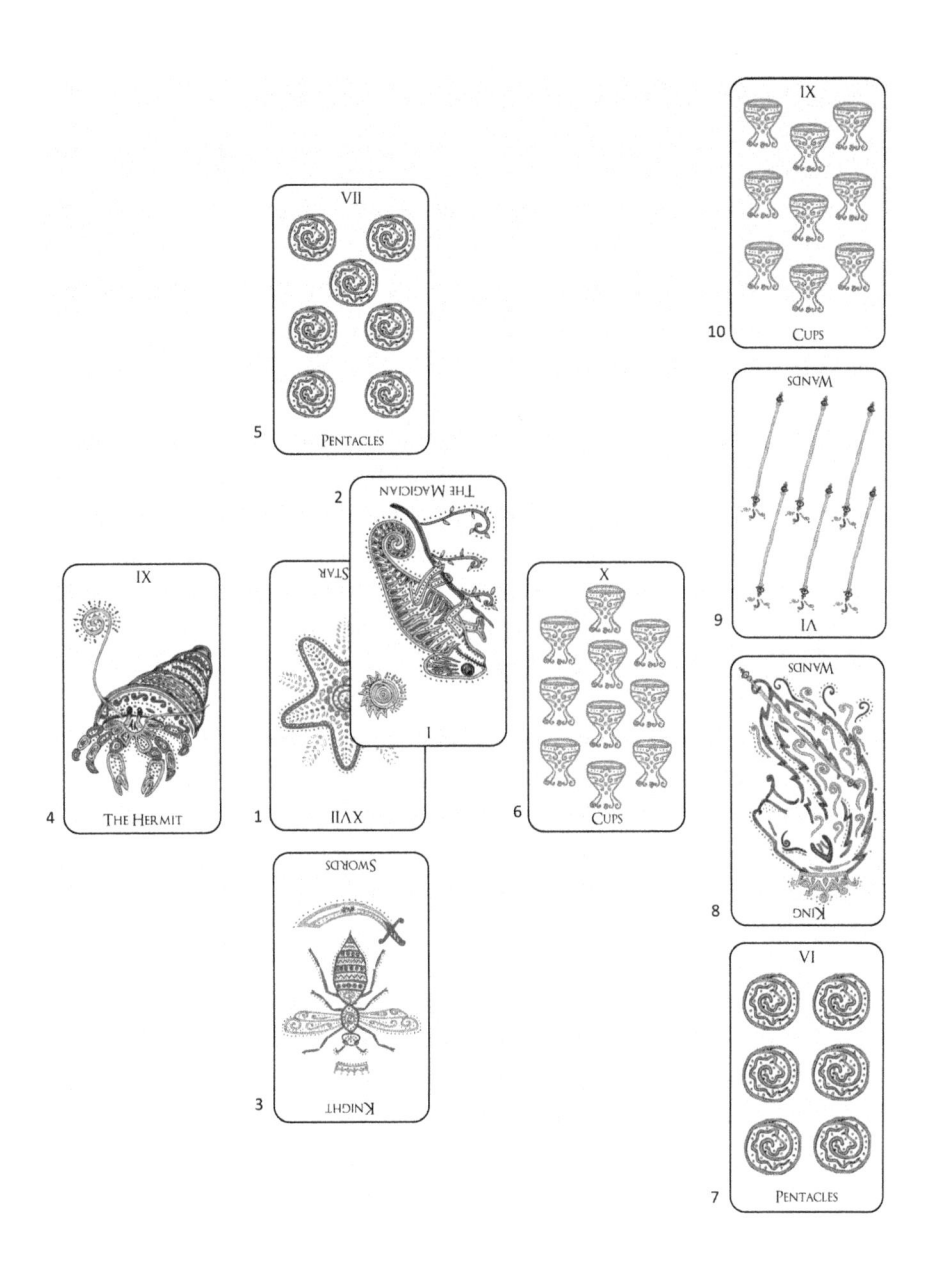

How I Would Interpret These Cards in a Reading

Katie came for a reading some time back wanting to know if she would every meet her Mr Right. She was longing for marriage and a family but it seemed as though it would never happen. She had been dating someone for six months and was wondering if this one would be the one. Was there any mileage in this relationship?

1: The Star Reversed as an issue. Katie was beginning to take a rather negative view of her worth in terms of relationships. She felt she was not pretty, talented or good enough for a potential mate. None of which is true as I found her to be very personable and nice looking. This made me think that her previous destructive relationships, including this one, had damaged the way she valued herself.

2: The Magician Reversed as what crosses her. In addition to negative self image above, she felt out of control and unable to steer her life in the direction she wanted. There is a feeling of powerlessness and maybe even defeatism attaching itself to this card when reversed. This does not mean it is true but just her skewed thinking on life.

3: Knight of Swords Reversed as the distant past. This would strongly point to a longer term relationship which failed and has caused her to carry forward unresolved issues from that time. I would suggest that this man must have let her down very badly and was probably verbally and emotionally bullying her thus causing her low self esteem.

4: The Hermit showed up in Katie's recent past. This points to a feeling of isolation and loneliness which one might expect to see in a person who was without a partner. The fact that she has a boyfriend alludes to the current relationship not being fulfilling and rather empty. Poor communication is very likely and he is probably emotionally unavailable. This does not help how she sees herself.

5: Seven of Pentacles for the near future. When it comes to finding a life long mate the likely scenario is that her present partner will prove to be hard work and she will wonder if he's worth the effort. I also felt that she was the one putting in the hard work when it was not reciprocated by her boyfriend.

6: Ten of Cups as the best possible outcome to hope for shows Katie can have what she desires and probably will as this is the wish card. True love is not out of reach but she will need to work for it and stop being defeatist about herself.

7: Six of Pentacles as how she is seen by others. This is often a card of doing good for others but putting yourself last. It sounds honourable, but Katie can be taken for a doormat and thus encourages losers and users to her door because she doesn't feel subconsciously she is worth any better.

8: King of Wands Reversed shows the other people in her life. This man is not for her, he will disappoint her and she is in danger of repeating a cycle of her past by choosing partners who take advantage of her and don't see her better qualities. She doesn't need to hang on to him simply because she is afraid of being alone. This is preventing a better man coming into her life.

9: Six of Wands Reversed as Katie's fears and worries. The card of victory i.e. achieving one's goals is reversed showing that she fears she will never succeed in her goal of being a happy married women with children. But this only a fear and a very destructive one because she doesn't realise all the wonderful qualities she has to offer a partner.

10: Nine of Cups as the ultimate outcome. This is a wonderful card to see as it does point to marriage, fulfilment and general happiness in a relationship and that things will go well in the future.

Although the outcome looked very bright, Katie needs to get from this point in time to the happy future foreseen by putting the effort in. Mr Perfect is not going to come knocking at her door unless she creates the right opportunities and starts to dig deep to find the confidence she once possessed before others trampled on her gentle and sensitive nature. She had some work to do but the Tarot indicated she would absolutely find the happiness she so deserved.

The Year Ahead Spread

Very simply, place one card or two for each month going forward to get a flavour for how your questioner's year will unfold. This is also highly effective doing it for 12 weeks ahead too if there is an issue to be resolved in the next few weeks. It must be remembered that nothing is set in stone in life and that things that may happen seven months down the line may well have started to happen at six months and might continue on to eight months. The timing spread gives a very good flavour for what is to happen but should not be read as absolute. As well as describing what is to happen I would also give a general overview at the end of the reading to highlight the most important months.

I have done this spread for myself in the past and written down the cards to refer back to. It is remarkable how accurate the cards are in hindsight - but whether we can also take their advice going forward is a different matter!

1: one month (or week) ahead

2: two months (or weeks) ahead

and so on.

13: three cards for a summary of the year or 12 weeks ahead.

Reading For Others   83

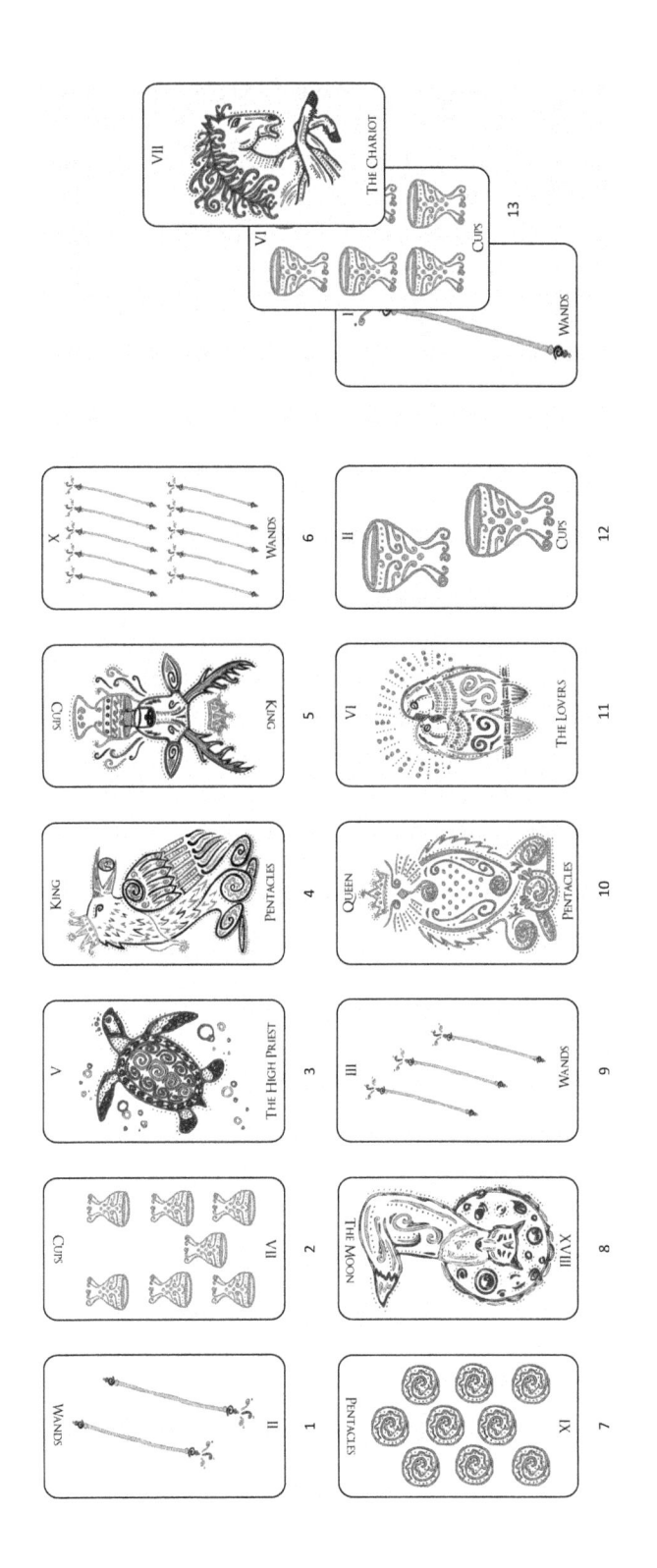

How I Would Interpret These Cards in a Reading

Adam wanted to know how his coming year would unfold. It was early February when I did his 12 month spread, following a difficult time during the previous year. He wanted to know if his idea of starting his own business would work as he was feeling very depressed about his current job. He also wanted to know if he would find new love after a painful breakup.

1: Two of Wands Reversed to represent February. It would seem that his doubt and confusion over his career and way ahead will still be prevalent this month. He is in some sort of inertia and lacking in drive right now.

2: Seven of Cups Reversed to represent March. This is a good card when reversed and I would have been more concerned if it were upright as it would show his self employment dreams were just that. However in the reversed , this shows Adam was becoming grounded and realistic about what was needed to carry his plans through. I felt he would start planning properly.

3: Hierophant to represent April. I thought this would be an excellent time for Adam to take advice from a business mentor and start really putting his plans into action. He also needed perhaps to further educate himself about running a business.

4: King of Pentacles to represent May. He would seem to be looking at his finances and what it might cost to start up on his own. Fortunately as the card is upright it seemed to suggest he would be taking good advice from a finance professional.

5: King of Cups Reversed to represent June. So far so good, but now we hit an obstacle in his progress. It is likely there may be some conflict with others, particularly his father (remember this could also be his mother). His father is well meaning and affectionate but too cautious in nature to agree this is a good step for Adam. His father may say it is too risky to support him.

6: Ten Wands to represent July. Adam appears to have entered a temporary trough. It may be that his confidence was knocked by his father's dissension and the realisation of what it takes to start a new business along with the risk is making him feel very burdened with doubt and discouragement.

7: Nine of Pentacles Reversed to represent August. The emphasis here is too much on money. Adam needs to come away from worrying about money to the extent it is preventing him from moving forward. He is clearly prevaricating because he is lacking confidence in himself. I would suggest this has its roots in well meaning but unhelpful advice from his father.

8: The Moon Reversed to represent September. This would suggest to me that there is some sort of catalyst to come which will propel Adam into his longed for business. I would hope that this is not redundancy but more likely to be he will discover he is being unfairly treated at work. There may be deception or lies around him that will help him decide enough is enough.

9: Three of Wands to represent October. Finally it would seem he will take the plunge around now and start up on his own. At the very least it indicates a new job if not a new business but whatever the career change it will be most welcome.

10: Queen of Pentacles to represent November. This shows me that having made the decision to move he will feel much more relaxed and grow in both maturity and financial sense. The other meaning is that he may meet a woman through the course of his work who may have a big part to play in his life.

11: The Lovers to represent December. If the lady he meets in November does not turn out to be the love of his life, he can be sure she is on her way in December. This strongly indicates that around this time he will meet someone new and enjoy a heady romance straight away.

12: Two of Cups to represent January. In a year's time, Adam can be assured he will have met with someone who he will really respect and fall in love. This could not have been a better ending to his year.

13: Ace of Wands, Six of Cups, The Chariot to represent a summary of the year to come. These are all extremely positive cards and nicely demonstrate what he can expect. The Ace of Wands points to a new beginning particularly in the professional sense, the Six of Cups points to his using his previously learnt skills and applying them for his own growth, it also shows the eventual support of his well meaning family. The Chariot not only shows a bumpy journey but with a victorious outcome but also refers to cars and other motors as well which I thought was highly relevant.

XX
Judgement

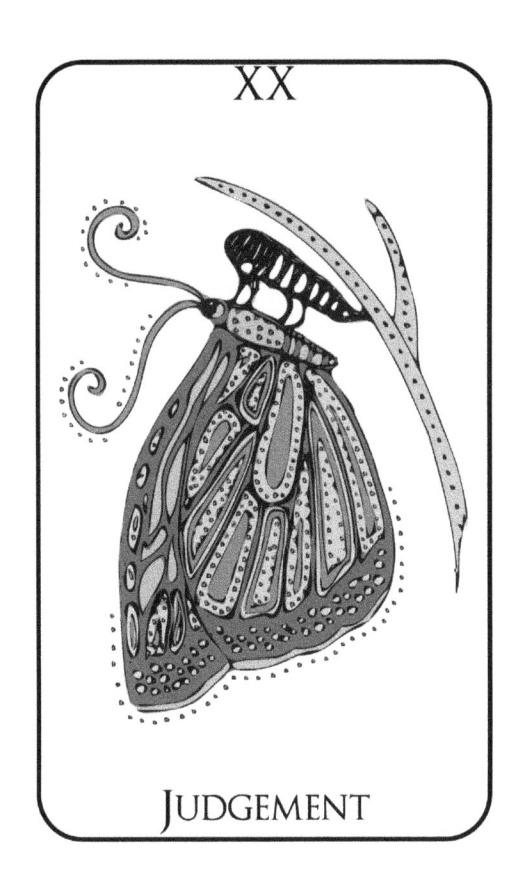

Relationship Spread

The majority of readings are about relationships so it is as well to have a spread dedicated to getting more insight to an existing or past affair. This spread, of course, can be applied to any relationship where your questioner needs to get a better understanding of the other person's point of view.

You will need to lay the cards out in two separate cross shapes - one representing you and one your partner (or other person).

Lay the cards out as the numbering suggests on the diagram - one card on your side, then one on theirs, back to one on your side then over to lay a card of their side again until all 15 cards are laid out.

1: The questioner's current situation

2: The partner's current situation

3: The background/distant past of the questioner's situation

4: The background/distant past of the partner's situation

5: The questioner's recent past and how they felt

6: The partner's recent past and how they felt

7: The questioner's near future and how they will feel

8: The partner's near future and how they will feel

9: Problems, fears and concerns to be overcome by questioner

10: Problems, fears and concerns to be overcome by partner

11: Events likely to occur for the questioner

12: Events likely to occur for the partner

13: Three cards for the likely outcome for both partners

YOU　　　　　　　　　　　　　　YOUR PARTNER

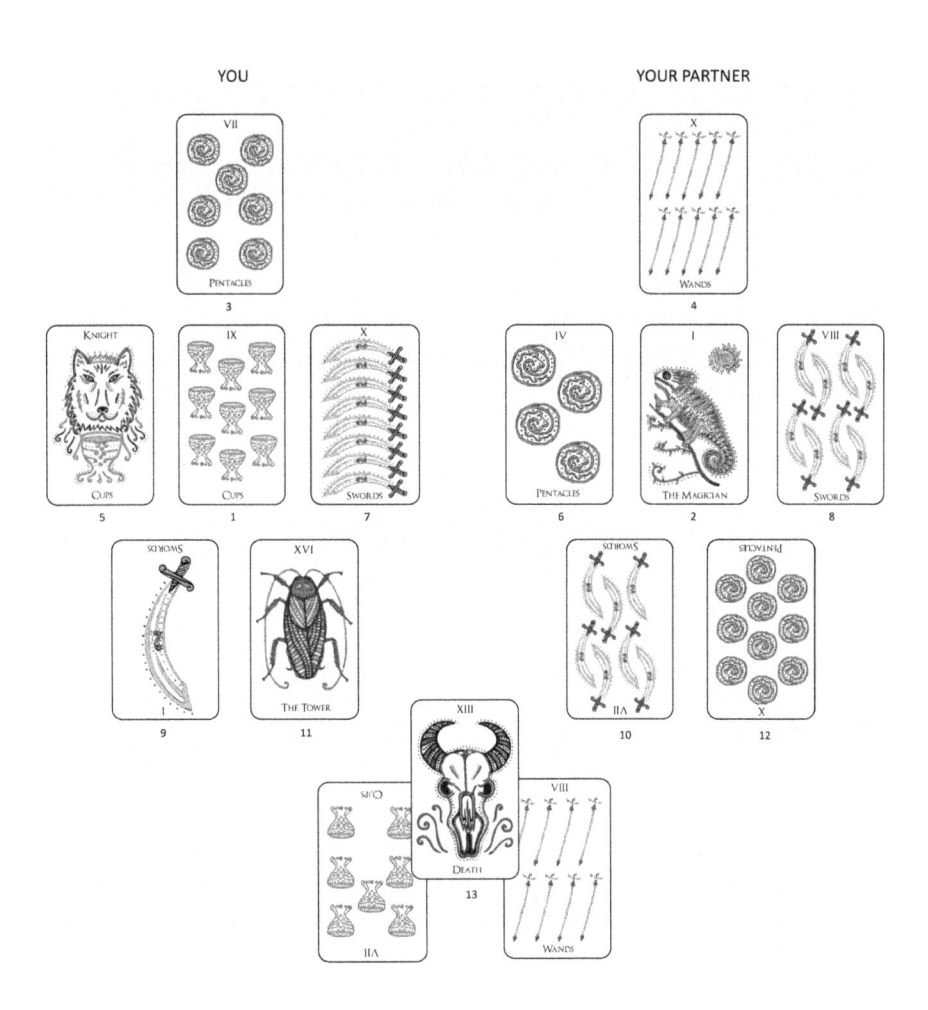

Reading For Others   89

How I Would Interpret These Cards in a Reading

Joanne came for a reading as she was concerned about where her relationship was heading. She has been in this relationship for just over a year and wanted to know how her boyfriend was feeling and thinking about their partnership as she intuitively felt things were not going too well. She said she didn't want anything sugar coated but would I please be honest in what I saw.

1: Nine of Cups as the questioner's current situation. This indicates that Joanne is looking for marriage or at least a long term committed relationship. She has the maturity and is at a time in her life when she feels this would be appropriate. Possibly she has projected this on to her current boyfriend and is trying to make him fit into the role of husband.

2: The Magician showing her boyfriend's current situation. The Magician is all about control and wants to be in charge of his own destiny. I am already feeling that Joanne's boyfriend is calling all the shots here and she is having to tow the line.

3: Seven of Pentacles shows Joanne's attitude towards the relationship from the start. Although she has found it hard work to make this work she felt if she tried hard enough she would be rewarded further down the line presumably by feeling she had won his heart.

4: Eight of Wands indicates her boyfriend's attitude from the start. He rushed into this relationship and was presumably infatuated and enjoyed the newness and excitement of it all.

5: Knight of Cups shows Joanne's feelings in the recent past. She was feeling that after this length of time they either make a commitment or not. She has very much hoped he would propose to her and still believes this can work.

6: Four of Pentacles shows her boyfriend's prevailing attitude over recent times. He is far too concerned about money and losing it. Maybe any discussions about engagement and marriage sound just too expensive. Perhaps this is his cover reason for stalling such a decision.

7: Ten of Swords for Joanne's near future. This does not bode well as it shows a feeling of being stabbed in the back and betrayed. This could either be her feelings and effort in the relationship being betrayed or worse that he is looking elsewhere for romantic company. (Be very careful of relaying news like this - I wouldn't give that suspicion unless she herself was suspicious and directly asked about his fidelity).

8: Eight of Swords shows her boyfriend's attitude in the near future could find him feeling trapped, looking for a way out.

9: Ace of Swords Reversed shows Joanne's fears and worries. Very simply this would show that the passion and vigour in the relationship is fading and whatever they had, they don't seem to have any more. She worries this is fizzling out.

10: Seven of Swords Reversed shows her boyfriend's concerns. This is not so much of a concern but adds further fuel to the fire that he is being deceptive towards her - in the very least his feelings. He is going through the motions in the relationship.

11: The Tower for future events is very explanatory. Joanne should not expect this relationship to last and in fact he may well end it because this is not indicating that she would do so. It will be very upsetting and soul destroying but out of the ashes new beginnings come.

12: Ten of Pentacles Reversed for his future events shows me that her boyfriend is far too concern about money and other practicalities to be worried about the two of them. His mind is elsewhere and he is likely to behave in a mean and nasty way.

13: Death, Seven of Cups Reversed, Ten of Wands as a summary and a guide to the outcome. It is already very obvious that this relationship is failing and won't last much longer. Death indicates sudden change which can be hard to deal with in the short term but long term is very much in her favour. This young man was not worthy of her affections. The Seven of Cups Reversed shows that she will be coming to her senses soon and seeing things as they really are. A realisation will dawn. Ten of Wands shows continued burdens until this sorry situation is at an end.

Additionally, it is worth noting there were three Tens in the whole reading which shows the end of a difficult and painful cycle and that Joanne is on the cusp of new and much brighter beginnings. The two Eights in his part of the spread indicate that he is the one in full control and has the upper hand which is further compounded by the Magician at the front. There was also an absence of any Cups for emotions on his side but more Pentacles than anything else.

This wasn't what she wanted to hear and it is very difficult as a reader to give such a downbeat and negative prospect but these are the cards she got and she didn't seem very surprised. After something like this, I would also offer to see what the future held in terms of fulfilment and happiness for Joanne. It turned out that a new romance was in the offing but that she'd have to wait a few months before this came into being.

Doubling Up

I have always used the method of doubling up the cards on each position - some readers I know even use treble cards for more illumination on an issue.

This works very well for me as it does give depth and more information to work on in a reading. In the general spread, I put down one card in both positions 1 and 2 and then two cards for each subsequent position until I reach position 8 which is the outcome. Here I lay five cards down simply because it gives a flavour for what is to come in the future. It really is up to you, the reader, to find your own style and preferred way of doing things.

Examples of Doubling Up versus Single Cards

Let us say that a Five of Swords is placed in position 4 - the recent past (as in the Fail Safe General Spread).

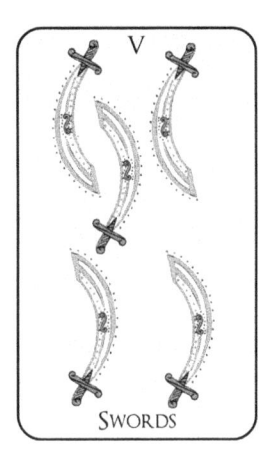

This would immediately tell you there had been quarrels, conflict and in the worse case scenario, violence. It may also mean the questioner has been facing some inner conflict and repressed feelings of anger, in other words the conflict may be internal rather than external.

Now let us add to the Five of Swords, another card in the doubled up method, this time it is the Eight of Cups

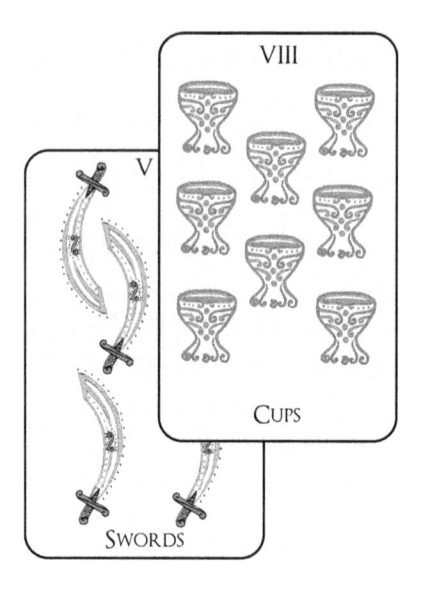

Reading the cards together now tells me that there has been conflict and anger but that the questioner's attitude is to walk away from the situation. They may already have done so. This is beginning to look like a relationship either family or romantic which has been under great pressure and may have fractured or broken down. Because of the position of the cards - the recent past - it doesn't indicate the future so you can be reasonably sure this has already happened or the questioner has decided on a course of action.

I hope this demonstrates that doubling up the cards offers depth to each position in the spread. If, in the course of reading, you feel you still need further clarity, then add other cards to the position in question. Say you wished to find out more information and you drew the Two of Cups, then it would relate to a romantic relationship. If you drew a court card (particularly if it is reversed) then this may still be the break down of a romantic relationship but it is much more likely to be a spouse, close friend or family member.

In this next example, imagine the first card drawn is the Lovers in Position 5 - the near future (as in the Fail Safe General Spread).

Super! It means that if our questioner is not attached at present, they will soon meet someone new and form a romantic attachment. If they are already in a relationship then there is a lot of love and affection within it. On the face of it, this looks good.

Now let's add another card in the doubling up method and this one is the Four of Pentacles reversed.

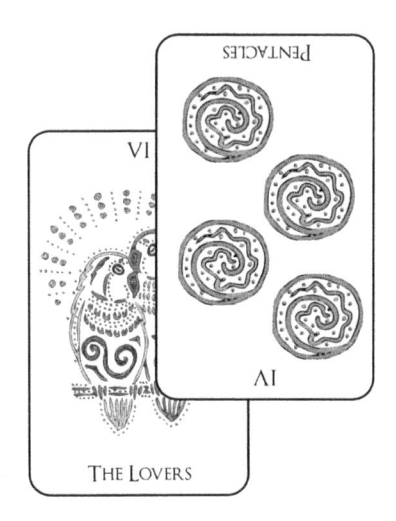

Reading For Others   95

This would be a note of caution. The Four of Pentacles reversed certainly points to financial loss or hardship. I would interpret this as our questioner needing to be very cautious in his or her new relationship that the person they become involved with does not bleed them dry of money. It is easy to be dazzled by a new partner and overlook the red flags. The questioner needs to examine their new partner's motives for getting involved - in this case money. If this is an established relationship, I would see this as a person being so enamoured by their partner but they are allowing money to drain away or feel powerless to do anything about it.

So the second card has added depth to the interpretation but also a warning. As with anything negative, tread carefully so as not to frighten or upset your questioner.

The Ethics of Reading for Others

This is really as important as any other subject in Tarot if not more so if you are intending to read for anyone other than yourself. I have discovered that Tarot card readings often effectively become counselling sessions. As a Tarot counsellor you must remember to listen carefully and not judge. Giving advice is an area you need to be very, very careful over. I have learnt that very often people take your throw away comments terribly seriously and you will want to avoid these coming back to bite you! Judging what you can and can't say will vary from individual to individual and you cannot apply a blanket style to all questioners. This is by far the hardest part of reading for others. Learning the meanings, remembering what it means to get several Threes in a spread, that's all well and good but your delivery of this information is the most important part.

Be Constructive

I had one sitter come to me for a reading who was visibly trembling with fear because a previous psychic had predicted a terrible accident. So powerful was this effect on her, it had ruined the quality of her life; she was terrified to get in a car or even walk down the street. I did what I could to tell her that psychics like those are charlatans and bring the art of Tarot into disrepute. I was able to calm her down and help her realise the prediction was entirely phoney and just a devise to get her to go back and spend more money with this so called psychic.

So whilst I'd like to think the vast majority of readers are well meaning, it is still easy to frighten your sitters unintentionally. This is why I consider the delivery and ethics part of a reading to be of the utmost importance area of Tarot to consider.

Don't Judge

Try to be compassionate and sensitive to your client's feelings even if what you hear shocks you. We all make mistakes and we all mess up from time to time because we are human and adversity is, sadly, unavoidable. Remind them that are completely normal. Also bear in mind that whilst it is tempting to believe wholesale everything a client has told you, people do tend to exaggerate and distort stories, it might be that their awful husband may not be as terrible as he is painted! Of course your client will want you to think you are on their side and it is appropriate you should be even when it's clear they haven't been as kind to others as they should have been. Also bear in mind there are always two sides to every story - I've often wondered what the absent and much maligned party would have to say. So delivering the news that the client might be at some way culpable for their situation has to be done sensitively and with great care.

No-Go Areas

Many people come seeking answers to highly emotive subjects and this has to be dealt with either with huge sensitively or not at all. My no-go areas are questions concerning chronic or serious illness such as cancer - I would always stress the client must act on their doctor's advice and maybe try some holistic therapies in addition. I absolutely will not answer questions on prognoses or predict outcomes in such circumstances. If a Tarot reader says you or your loved one will be fine where there is a medical diagnoses of serious illness, then this is very dangerous territory. Some impressionable people will think that's good enough and give up conventional treatment.

I am also highly reluctant to answer questions concerning fertility. This is a medical issue again and highly emotive - it'll put you into a very awkward position. If the question is "when will I get pregnant?" or "will this round of IVF work?" I'd be strongly inclined not to give a prediction either way because;

what if you say they won't get pregnant because it only shows disappointment in the cards - how upsetting would that be for a woman who is desperate for a child? Equally, if you tell her, yes you'll have a baby during this round of IVF and she doesn't - was it really worth raising her hopes so high only for them to be dashed? Have a sense of responsibility over what is suitable for Tarot or what's suitable for the doctor.

The Give-It-To-Me-Straight Types

I knew a reader whose questioner asked whether her husband was having an affair or not - I believe she said "give it to me straight as I need to know for sure". My reader friend reluctantly indicated that cards did indeed indicate his deception. Later on, my friend received a call from the questioner who said she was outside her husband's mistresses house with a shotgun. The questioner thanked the reader for providing the evidence she needed. I don't think anyone got hurt but clearly this situation is extreme and a really upsetting one for the reader. You need to be able to assess whether your questioner really does want the answer or not. Above all, try to remember how you would feel if you were told that your spouse is having an affair.

Even when people say they want it straight and need the truth, this may not be the case. They invariably will have a particular answer they want to hear and may not be as strong as they appear to be. If they seem very emotional I would proceed with the utmost caution.

Realistic Predictions - Not Wild ones

At the risk of contradicting the above, I need to turn now to being truthful in a reading. I endeavour to be honest in what I see and not give false hopes in order to keep the questioner happy, therefore, if the question is highly emotional such as "is my ex partner coming back to me?" make your client aware they may not receive the answer they want. When it comes to reigniting a love affair, I find that generally it doesn't happen and even if it does it tends not to last - you cannot control someone else's free will. That is speaking from experience of reading over the years. I think that if a relationship fails then there was a reason for that and, as hard as it is to accept, it probably just wasn't meant to be even if the questioner was convinced it was!

I do feel very sad for the heartbroken and hate to see what appears to be very obvious games which are played by the absent party which lead my questioners to feel there is a crumb of hope. I had a questioner recently who got quite upset when I was unable to confirm that there would be a happy reunion with an ex lover; she said to me "but the other Tarot reader I saw yesterday told me we'd get back together and we'd get married within the year". I couldn't see it in the cards and could only comment on what was in front of me. I feel that such wild predictions raise hope which can only be dashed to a devastating degree which would be irresponsible. Listening to the questioner's story, this was an abusive and controlling relationship which she was well out of, but that was my opinion. She was looking for a particular answer and I couldn't in all honesty give it. It did also occur to me that if the she had been convinced by the first reader she wouldn't have come to me for confirmation. I felt the questioner was depressed and urged her to seek medical advice.

Magic Dust

People often come to see me wanting reassurance that the future will be OK but what some don't realise is that they can control much of what happens in their lives. What a minority of clients want is to be told everything will work out fine - that they don't need to do a thing in order to achieve this, it's almost as though they perceive a Tarot reading acts like magic dust sprinkled over their problems for an effortless, positive outcome. I do appreciate that we don't always want to face reality, we've all been there and it's hard sometimes to make ourselves see things as they really are. Again, it's all perfectly normal to be like this sometimes. But, like everything else in life, if it's worth having, it's worth working for. The cards just point the way and it's up to the questioner to fix what can be fixed and stop trying to fix what can't.

I always try to look for practical solutions to questioners' issues with help from the cards. I have found that there are no short cuts to what we want in life. The greatest satisfaction is when we achieve a goal through hard work. Is your client being carried with the river or are they swimming against the current? Either way, feeling out of control can be frightening, but I believe that life has a habit of resolving what appears unresolvable. We just have to give it a push sometimes.

A Two Way Process

Tarot readings are a two way process. I can and often do ask questions during a reading and look for the client's involvement in the reading. This helps the cards to give up more information and thus we can focus on their very unique issues which go beyond the scope of the general meanings of the cards. Some clients believe that one can see all sorts of things in the cards which they really don't offer up. For example a lady I read for recently was excited about the prospect that new love was coming into her life. However, she wanted to know more about this future man she hasn't met yet. How tall he was, his ethnicity, his profession, the colour of his eyes and his age. Well, the profession is the easiest to discern but for the rest of it, I would have been guessing.

The best readings are those where the questioner has come with an idea of the questions they'd like answers to. Sometimes I get a questioner who is "just curious" or doesn't have anything they want to ask about. These readings tend to be very short as it's true to say that if your life is going pretty well at the moment then not much will come out of a reading. Tarot works very well if you are looking for guidance on a relationship, work, family and so on.

Unfortunately, some clients come hoping to be impressed with "magic tricks" and try to test me to see if I can read their minds or see into their lives. This tends to happen more at parties, especially where people are drinking and see Tarot as a bit of a laugh. I tend now to find out what the general attitude is towards Tarot before I'll undertake parties of people.

I have also had clients who stare at me blankly with folded arms waiting to be amazed at my psychic powers whilst barely uttering a word or even giving a smile. My card reading abilities are very much enhanced if I have made a positive connection with the client. This does not mean that they should tell me everything up front - I would rather not know anything about my client first when I do my general reading at the start so as not to be influenced by prior knowledge. I am often surprised at how accurate the cards are in the initial spread.

The Structure of the Reading

So my process is like this; I start with a general spread to see what comes up and it's not always what a client thinks it might be. There can be one overall theme, such as their relationship, or it can throw up a number of different and apparently unconnected areas of their lives, however, there is usually a link somewhere down the line.

As I conclude the general spread, I do further spreads so that we can then focus on the issues they would like to explore. For example, if they are thinking of changing their job but are worried about what might happen if they do, then this is the time during the reading to look at that. There is usually plenty to talk about during the 40-45 minute reading.

Overall, quite a significant majority of people come for readings when they are stuck in their lives or very unhappy. They will sometimes tell you things that they have never told anyone before and sometimes they weep. So I hardly need reiterate the importance of employing tact, empathy and a non judgemental attitude. The greatest pleasure for a reader comes in lifting someone's spirits or as someone recently said to me "I'll sleep better tonight. Thank you."

Disclaimer

I would advise that you give a disclaimer on your website if you have one in order to cover yourself in the event of a disgruntled client. The other benefit of this, (providing anyone actually reads it!) is that it may give people a realistic idea of what to expect. We really don't want questioners to turn up expecting the end-of-pier gypsy in a beaded headscarf experience. I would hope that the points below will sort out those who are serious about a Tarot reading from those who think it's a bit of fun.

Here are some ideas for a disclaimer:

- A Tarot reading is subject to the my interpretation and your understanding of what is said and should not be taken as absolute. I cannot guarantee the accuracy of a reading and I cannot guarantee I can always give you specific answers to questions.

- A Tarot reading does not absolutely predict the future but is based on the probable outcome of events which can be influenced by your future actions or attitude.

- I am a Tarot reader with some mediumistic ability, however, I cannot guarantee to make connection with those who have passed over, nor will I try to connect to any one person in spirit.

- I am not a mind reader nor can I see into your life.

- A Tarot reading does not replace professional medical, legal, personal, business or any other advice that I am not professionally qualified for.

- I do not predict the lotto numbers.

- I do not give medical diagnoses or prognoses which includes IVF treatment.

- Any decisions made or actions taken by you as a result of your Tarot reading are your sole responsibility. I will offer my opinion and advice, but will not interfere with your free will. I will not coerce you to follow a particular course of action, or attempt to exert any form of control over your free will.

- I assume no legal liability for any damages, losses, or other consequences of any decisions, subsequent to, or based on my Tarot readings.

- A Tarot reading is a two way process. I will ask questions and expect your involvement during your reading.

- Tarot cards are not dangerous or in anyway carry negative vibrations. They are pieces of card with imagery on which is interpreted by the Tarot reader.

- To avoid disappointment or an unnecessary Journey, a pre-arranged appointment is essential. I cannot accommodate those who call unexpectedly, either in person or over the phone looking for an immediate Tarot consultancy.

- I do not offer Tarot Readings to anyone under 18 years of age.

- All readings are completely private and confidential. I will not share them with a third party.

- I will never refuse a client a Tarot consultancy on the grounds of race, colour, religious belief, disability or sexual orientation.

- I do not invoke or remove spells or curses.

Card Meanings

Major Arcana

0 - The Fool

Upright: This is a card of beginnings and of journeys into the unknown. A new relationship or new course of action in life but one which is rushed into without caution. This is an exciting time of new adventure and expansion. Look before you leap and consider your actions to avoid making a fool of yourself.

Reversed: Rash or foolish behavior. Infatuation, unable to control emotions. Ill thought out actions resulting in failure. Fail to plan, plan to fail. This can represent other peoples' ignorant or stupid behavior which can result in causing oneself difficulties.

I - The Magician

Upright: A strong and positive card, the Magician represents creativity, self-reliance and awareness of abilities. Taking control and creating one's own path in life. New business, new venture and entrepreneurism all well starred here. Being bold, decisive and skilful - go for it!

Reversed: A feeling of being out of control in life. Not making use of talents and resources, underestimating one's worth. Being unduly influenced by others instead of self reliance, lack of confidence. Ill considered plan. Irresponsibility, missed opportunities. Don't be tricked or conned by others.

II - The High Priestess

Upright: Use of one's feminine energy regardless of gender. The High Priestess rules the unconscious, our spirituality and psychic ability. Learn to trust instincts more. Listen to gut instinct because it's correct in this instance. Find guidance through stillness and meditation.

Reversed: Refusal to see what is there, a denial of truth. Being in denial about something important, usually of their own spirituality. Being concerned only with material things and not listening to intuition which is trying to say something important. Fear of facing the unpalatable truth.

III - The Empress

Upright: The Empress represents Mother Earth and abundant fruitfulness. It can show pregnancy, conception or even longing for a baby. She is the essence of motherhood expressed in nurturing and compassion but also in sexuality and femininity. Creating a beautiful home and garden.

Reversed: Difficulties in conceiving, unwanted pregnancy, dissatisfaction with one's home or lot in life. Needing to be out in nature but feeling cut off from it. This could even represent problems with one's Mother. It may also show issues in accepting one's femininity or sexuality. Sexual difficulties.

IV - The Emperor

Upright: Here is a Father or other person in authority such as a boss. This means structure and order is needed in life in order to function well. Time to face up to responsibilities. As a person the Emperor is reliable, strong and independent. He's in charge but loyal and utterly trustworthy.

Reversed: An arrogant bully, aggressive and unpleasant. It can represent loss of control, lack of discipline and resistance to authority. This can show a man who has been weakened either physically or mentally. A feeling of being emasculated and undermined. Frustration and anger.

V - The Hierophant

Upright: The path to success lies in following tradition rather than the unconventional. Steadfastness, dependability and conformity are all hallmarks of this card. A mentor or educator is shown here. Work within education or even a religion is indicated. It's time to continue one's learning.

Reversed: A person who has led an unstructured life and is lacking in formal education. It may also represent the desire to live in an unconventional style. A person who rejects their background and culture and has issues with conformity. Atheism. Being too kind to others and being taken advantage of.

VI – The Lovers

Upright: Either a new relationship is shown or love and passion will be coming into one's life. If already in a relationship, it shows renewed passion. Lovers reunited. Relationships in general will go very well. At the very least it can mean the blossoming of friendship. Family love and devotion.

Reversed: Unrequited love or a relationship which is fading. It can indicate a parting of ways. It might also refer to infatuation which can be easily confused with love. A difficult choice is to be made but the decision is hard. Being tied to the wrong person for the wrong reasons. The end of a relationship.

VII – The Chariot

Upright: Life's journey is, and will be, bumpy for a while but the outcome will be well worth it. The road is rough and challenging but the result will be good. There may be a move of home or problems with vehicles. Possibly travel or a young person going off to university or further education.

Reversed: The road is going to be rocky for some time yet, no end in sight for difficulties, but no matter how stressful, nothing lasts forever. Problems arising not of the questioner's choosing but by others. Problems with vehicles breaking down and delays on journeys.

VIII - Strength

Upright: This card can mean physical or emotional strength. If a person has been feeling ill or even depressed, this card would indicate a return of vitality. Strength is also quiet courage and stoicism in the face of adversity. Getting on with things. Trust in one's own strength.

Reversed: A person who is weakened through adversity or ill health. Can indicate depression or illness and a need for recuperation. This is also a warning not to let others undermine your strengths and take advantage. Lack of courage, cowardice and underhand behaviour also indicated.

IX - The Hermit

Upright: This shows the need to spend some time contemplating what is wanted out of life and to start planning ahead. An importance decision lies ahead. The Hermit shows the way forward. Follow a spiritual path and learn to trust the answer to all is already within. Meditate.

Reversed: This card can indicate loneliness, isolation or obsessive thoughts about an issue. Being abandoned and rejected leading to childish or petulant behaviour. Refusal to allow others to help when one would benefit from support.

X - Wheel of Fortune

Upright: Indicates that life is changing beyond one's control. A stroke of luck or unusual occurrence will happen which can change circumstance out of the blue. Nothing stays the same forever. A fluid situation liable to change. Take advantage of new opportunities which are presented.

Reversed: Possibly a reversal in fortune, some unexpected negative event setting life back temporarily. Challenges ahead may need to be met with courage and fortitude. As with the upright meaning, nothing lasts for ever. Temporary setbacks.

XI - Justice

Upright: Legal issues to be resolved from court cases, compensation, conveyancing to making a will. Outcomes to legal matters look very positive. Justice will be served. Can also mean Justice in the wider sense; fairness and balance. Marriage and business partnerships will go very well.

Reversed: A miscarriage of justice, unfairness and imbalance. Court cases may not be resolved satisfactorily. Legal action taken against one. Perhaps an unfair accusation or treatment. A lack of promotion at work possibly underhand politics.

XII - The Hanged Man

Upright: Life in the balance, this card often means a person is hanging in limbo, can't go back or move forward. Good things to come after adversity. Things are stagnating and feels like nothing will ever change but there is a turning point to come soon. Can indicate shoulder, back or knee problems.

Reversed: The feeling of stagnation will last a while longer. A difficult situation must be endured and patience is needed whilst realising not everything can be controlled. Don't put up with a poor situation, such as a dead end relationship, simply because it's the easy way. Objective thinking is needed.

XIII - Death

Upright: A positive card as it means change. Death of the old self leading to rebirth of the new. Clearing the path of old, worn out relationships, jobs or other major parts of life to make way for new and better times ahead. Change can be hard to go through but is always for the better in the longer term.

Reversed: Difficult and sweeping changes are softened when this card is reversed. But certainly change is still predominant here. A general malaise or lethargy is indicated as is depression. Overall this is positive as bad influences are on the way out.

XIV - Temperance

Upright: Peaceful, harmonious times lie just ahead. If life has been fraught, calmer waters are shown here. This card urges moderation in all things; eat well, drink less alcohol, give up smoking etc. If one has been feeling in a hurry to get things moving, be patient. Be calm. It will come at the right time.

Reversed: This can mean impatience and a feeling that things are not happening quickly enough. The questioner is trying to influence events by speeding things up. It can mean being too busy and not taking time to relax which is needed. Also substance abuse can be indicated here - time to cleanse.

XV - The Devil

Upright: The Devil ties us to a job, a house or a person who is no longer good for us - if they ever were! It is about enslavement or bondage, being tied or imprisoned when it's hard to break free. Sexual obsession and unhealthy relationships. Sever these bonds now and break free of evil people.

Reversed: Very much like the upright meaning but the influence is passing quickly. The questioner may short be able to break free of that which has enslaved them. There may be wicked or downright nasty people around the questioner. A warning not to get involved in anything illegal or evil.

XVI - The Tower

Upright: Loss, destruction and disaster can be indicated. It might show an unpleasant surprise is on the way. A feeling that life has pulled the rug from under one's feet. Illusions will be shattered and an unhappy truth will emerge. After this a better life will emerge.

Reversed: It can also show more of a long term misery rather than a sudden catastrophe, or the after effects of a disaster which one is still living with. Problems are not yet solved, there may be oppression. The questioner will need to make a big effort to overcome difficulties and not drown in them.

XVII - The Star

Upright: The Star of Hope. Optimism and good luck in abundance. After a difficult time things will go very well. Recovery from illness and general good fortune in jobs, relationships and all other areas of life. Often connected to travel and beneficial education. Life enhancing experiences on the way.

Reversed: A watered down version of the above, there is still reason for hope but possibly the questioner is refusing to look on the positive side of things. It can also indicate where talents and abilities are not being used or have been dismissed by others. Pessimism is likely.

XVIII - The Moon

Upright: Deception, trickery and deceit are indicated. Something being deliberately hidden. Can show lies are being told. Insincerity and trouble makers and general frustrating delays in information are indicated. Listen to doubts, all is not what it seems, learn to trust instinct.

Reversed: Similar to the above meaning but on a more minor scale. There will still be deception and lies around. This card reversed can show the cards are not willing to reveal more about a situation. Try again later. Can be connected to poor life choices and substance abuse. Mental illness.

XIX - The Sun

Upright: A glorious card. Happiness, joy and good times ahead. Strongly associated with children and the arrival of a longed for baby. Exuberance and fun in the future. A forthcoming marriage will be happy and long. Recovery from illness. General good fortune and positivity. A good omen.

Reversed: There is potential for great happiness but something has knocked the shine off life a little at the moment. Problems concerning children and conception. Marriage difficulties but with work can be overcome. All problems are resolvable with work and a positive attitude.

XX - Judgement

Upright: Freedom from restraints, bursting free from old life into better times. A positive legal outcome and release from the bonds of the past. Time to look back and assess what has been achieved and make peace with oneself. Retirement, or a new and positive phase in life. Rebirth.

Reversed: This still refers to endings but the outcomes may not be very satisfactory. The questioner may feel guilty about their behaviour or know they could have done better. Some selfishness is showing here. Legal matters are also not showing in a positive light here.

XXI - The World

Upright: Success, a raise or praise. Expansion of oneself. The World shows rewards for hard efforts and projects in the future will go very well. A marriage or new job are well starred with this card. Often connected to travel or emigration. Life enhancing experiences due to seeing the World.

Reversed: Becoming stuck in a rut and being unwilling to make positive changes. The inability to accept change even when it is very necessary. This can point to jealousy also and feeling one's own progress in life has not been as good as others. Keep trying and be patient is the message.

Minor Arcana

Wands

Ace of Wands

Upright: New beginnings or a new enterprise, perhaps a new job or a job offer is on the way. Occasionally this card represents the birth of a child. In my experience it tends to relate to business, projects and creativity. Putting one's ideas into action and having a successful start. Good business idea.

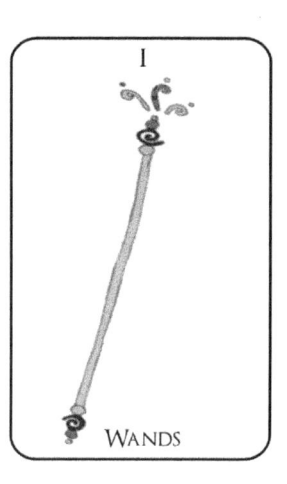

Reversed: The potential for a new job or new business enterprise is possible, but further action is needed by the questioner to bring it to fruition. Also a new job or business which will have problems attached and may cause anxiety. Difficulties with conceiving a child.

Two of Wands

Upright: This can mean indecision or a choice of two different courses of action particularly in matters of work or business. Often indicates the formation of a business partnership. A strong and positive card, this can mean that you have found the right person for the job. Be decisive.

Reversed: Stagnation and delays in making decisions. Being completely stuck over a choice. Business partnerships are not well starred here. Extreme caution needed before coming to an important decision.

Three of Wands

Upright: I nearly always find this card relates to a new job or that a new career is on the horizon. For someone who does not work, this can mean a new project or the desire to find pastures new, even travel is shown here. Either way, this person does not wish to stand still or accept the status quo.

Reversed: The potential for a new job is here but yet to be acted on. It may mean job rejections and show a period of hard work in order to get where the questioner wants to be. Travel plans may face delays. The desire to move forward in life is temporarily suspended.

Four of Wands

Upright: Connected to the home, perhaps a move of house or even just renovations which will be a boost to all concerned. This is a card of putting down roots and the desire for a change of residence. Time to relax and look back at all you've achieved and feel proud. Sometimes means hidden musical talent!

Reversed: Can mean a move of house is beset by problems or delayed. Problems or upheavals in the home or the inability to decide on whether to put down roots or not. Try another time.

Five of Wands

Upright: This cards shows a struggle in the matter of negotiation. This can mean difficulty in making your opinions heard or getting others to understand your position. Someone may not be listening to you despite your best efforts. Business matters may be delayed or put off for the time being.

Reversed: This negative influence should be passing soon. With effort, one's point of view can be put across and understood. A rift may soon be healed.

Six of Wands

Upright: Victory or success of some sort is on the way. Often in relation to business or work matters for example winning a big contract. Negotiations will go well and legal battles will go in your favour. You are the victor and about to taste the rewards of your hard work.

Reversed: A hollow victory or partial success but clouded by not being complete. There may be a big obstacle ahead so it might be worth leaving this issue alone for the time being. Others may cause trouble.

Seven of Wands

Upright: Stand your ground over a certain matter despite challenges to your authority of decision making. One problem after another to be overcome but you can do it. It feels like a constant battle but you will rise up above the stress and show the rest of the world your true mettle.

Reversed: The pressures and problems arising might overwhelm the questioner. Don't try to overcome them, better to walk away and try again later. Possibly an embarrassing situation may be about to occur unless one takes precautions to avoid this.

Eight of Wands

Upright: Matters rushing to a conclusion, whatever is going on, there will be swift activity and a quick resolution. Sometimes life moving too quickly and there is a need to slow things down. Travel is a definite possibility and having new experiences with new people. Possibly a new romance.

Reversed: Matters not moving fast enough for the questioner. Possibly this is a chance to assess if what is desired is really worth having. Impatience is indicated here. Sometimes jealousy is indicated by others towards the questioner.

Nine of Wands

Upright: Being stuck in a rut of doing things in a tried and trusted way - however this will not work for too much longer. Time to broaden your horizons and think outside the box in order to find the solution to a problem. Can indicate a person who is unwilling to change even though they are burdened.

Reversed: This shows a willingness for a person to change what they are doing to achieve positive results. Maverick behaviour but not in a negative way. Moving out of a burdened situation.

Ten of Wands

Upright: This shows a person who is very overburdened with worries and concerns. Others around maybe adding to these worries. This sort of pressure is hard to see past and can be very difficult to deal with, however this cycle of stress will not last forever - a new and better life cycle will soon start.

Reversed: Burdens, worries and concerns are definitely on the way out now. There is light at the end of the tunnel and soon the questioner will be able to move forward unfettered by previous problems. Just be patient a little while longer.

Page of Wands

Upright: Usually indicates a young person or child or a person with a childlike attitude. A talkative and irrepressible character, keen for new experiences whilst not afraid of a challenge. Watch out for opportunities which may soon present themselves. Go for it.

Reversed: Problems besetting a youngster. Difficulties at school or a need to watch them carefully in case of hidden worries and sadnesses. Delays or disappointments in business through a lack of opportunity.

Knight of Wands

Upright: A charming and likeable character, the Knight in this suit gets a long way on his or her personal charm. Indicates a youthful person or being youthful in outlook. Possible romance or business dealings with a real charmer. Someone who rushes in where angels fear to tread.

Reversed: Irresponsibility and immaturity are shown here. This person may be unreliable or worse, untrustworthy. The questioner may be disappointed in business or even by a romantic partner. This indicates being let down in some way.

Queen of Wands

Upright: This card, often refers to a woman and shows a reliable and honest person - the sort of friend you can rely upon when you are in a fix. This often relates to friendships and trust. She would make a super boss due to her friendly and open nature.

Reversed: This can show a person one once considered a friend is now pulling away. The end of a friendship possibly problems to do with jealousy. Possibly a female boss or someone in authority with an axe to grind. Difficult and petty behaviour.

King of Wands

Upright: A helpful and trustworthy character. This man is affectionate but I would stop short of describing him as loving. He (or she) is likely to be a mentor or a well-meaning boss. He has a good mind and plenty of life experience to draw on in order to give sound advice.

Reversed: This can mean the opposite of above. He (or she) might be dishonest and a liar. He has no good intentions towards the questioner being too self serving and narcissistic. He may make promises he is quite unable or unwilling to keep.

Cups

Ace of Cups

Upright: A new romance, falling in love. Meeting a soul mate or at the very least making positive new friendships. This indicates the people we love in general but is often connected to romance. Sometimes shows the birth of a child. A card of beginnings, newness and freshness.

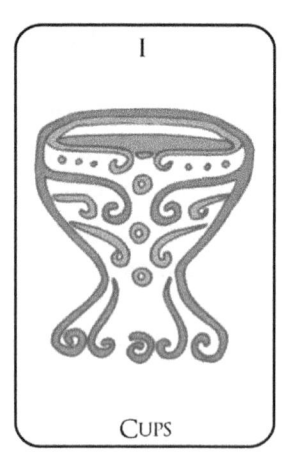

Reversed: Love may be on the way but perhaps not immediately, other events need to take place first before. Love could be fading - someone may not have their heart in the relationship anymore. Problems with fertility and conception but not impossible. There may a child in the future, just not now.

Two of Cups

Upright: A partnership often romantic. Two people falling in love and/or making a commitment to each other. An engagement or decision to live together. Romance will flourish. Even business partnerships can show here meaning real friendship and an excellent working relationship ahead.

Reversed: Possibly a parting of ways for a couple. This may only be temporary or it might prove permanent. This can also indicate where one partner is much more involved than the other or there is a reluctance to make a commitment somewhere down the line.

Three of Cups

Upright: Time to celebrate and enjoy family, friends and loved ones' company. Often shows when a celebration such as a wedding, christening or family party is coming. Fun and pleasant times ahead. An unexpected happy surprise. Accomplishments are recognised and rewarded.

Reversed: A desired marriage will not take place. Relationships that are superficial with no commitment and tend to indicate a "friends with benefits" situation. Cancelled engagements or parties. Possibly even divorce shown here.

Four of Cups

Upright: This shows dissatisfaction with one's lot even if it's not justified. Misery caused by ourselves by wanting what we can't have. A large advantage one has not yet noticed right under their nose. Advice is be careful not to miss a super opportunity whilst feeling sorry for yourself. Look around you.

Reversed: Reversing the above meaning, this means a person decides what they want out of life and takes advantage of opportunities presented. Being positive and decisive. New and happy experiences are on the way including new people.

Five of Cups

Upright: Sadness, misery and loss, possibly regretful feelings. Feeling sorry or even foolish over one's own actions. Contrition. All is not lost, please don't despair there is plenty to look forward to after a period of mourning or moping. Try and find optimism - this period is passing quickly.

Reversed: Watered down version of above. Feelings of sadness, loss and regret are already beginning to fade albeit they have left their mark. A glimpse of happiness to come and possibly even reuniting with people from the past.

Six of Cups

Upright: The card of the family. This shows devotion and duty and a generally happy family situation. It can sometimes indicate when family life can carries its duties and responsibilities. Also means reaching into one's past in order to find the way forward. Old talents and skills put to good use.

Reversed: Problems besetting the family. Families at loggerheads or even not talking to each other. The loss of a figurehead which has affected the other members of the family very adversely. A lack of support from family, the questioner will have to stand on their own two feet from now on.

Seven of Cups

Upright: Foolish fantasy, living with one's head in the clouds and failing to see life as it really is. Escapism from reality. Clutching at straws in a hopeless situation and refusing to face facts. There is a need to be grounded and face the music. Groundless optimism - you're missing something.

Reversed: Becoming grounded and taking a more realistic view of life. This indicates practicality and a person who is not afraid to face the truth. Any problems will be resolved soon. Pragmatism.

Eight of Cups

Upright: The need to walk away from a situation which has run its course. Overwhelming desire to escape the present situation. Looking over one's shoulder and thinking "is it worth one last try?" The answer is no. Walk towards the light at the end of the tunnel. It's over and you need to start anew.

Reversed: This speeds up the above meaning. There is definitely a much more encouraging situation and future showing itself now. It means that a person has already walked away from their problems and is moving away from a horrible situation once and for all.

Nine of Cups

Upright: Success and satisfaction with life. Life will go well materially and emotionally. This card shows a comfortable and financial stable marriage may be on the way particularly for an older person. Time to take stock of all you have achieved in life and to feel good about your successes big or small.

Reversed: There is partial success here. This is such a positive card there is not much negative about it. A marriage will take place but not just yet. It can show successes but perhaps not as great as anticipated.

Ten of Cups

Upright: This is sometimes called the "wish" card. Start wishing as you may well get what you ask for. A tremendously happy card; marriage, children, work; all things will go well. Great card for a new romance. Happiness, joy and contentment with warm and loving relationships.

Reversed: As above but not quite as strong. Happiness and romance will come but may take a little longer to materialise or there may be some small and irritating difficulties to overcome.

Page of Cups

Upright: Often a young person or child, showing a quiet, loving, reflective nature. In an older person, maturity is lacking and the need to grow up. Also mean young love. A good card if you're unsure if someone has feelings towards you - they do.

Reversed: Problems with a child, emotionally or educationally. Young person may not be applying themselves as well as they might leading to concerns over school or college work. Exams might be failed. Behavioural problems might erupt. Take the time to find out the underlying reasons.

Knight of Cups

Upright: An honourable and reliable young person with an open heart. In an older person a sense of retained youthfulness in appearance and manner. A romantic proposal can be indicated here, or at least a love interest coming forward into one's life. Even a work proposal is possible.

Reversed: Possibly romance is fading. The questioner may be let down or disappointed in love. A much wanted engagement is not going to happen and there might even be deception or unfaithfulness at work here. An unreliable person.

Queen of Cups

Upright: A loving and caring person, nurturing and gentle. The Queen represents maturity and the blossoming of the feminine side of a person. She is no fool however and sees through people when they are deceptive. An excellent judge of character and sensitive to people's feelings.

Reversed: She can be spoiled and selfish and a bit of a drama queen. Either that or she withholds her feelings and affection due to having been disappointed in love or even emotionally rejected as a child. She may be facing rejection in the near future. She might have feelings of jealousy.

King of Cups

Upright: A loving parental figure. A person who has grown in strength by using compassion. A person who exercises control with kindness and love rather than discipline. Has let people run rings around him at times but his heart is in the right place. An exceptionally affectionate person.

Reversed: He might be self centred and unable to give love freely due to selfishness or rejection he has suffered in the past. He could be possessive and jealous; a difficult partner to live with. He might be losing interest in his relationship.

Pentacles

Ace of Pentacles

Upright: A new opportunity usually associated with a new job. It can be a raise or praise in connection with work but there is certainly money coming towards you. It may be money right out of the blue; it'll feel like a gift from the heavens. Mostly I've seen this card in connection to career matters.

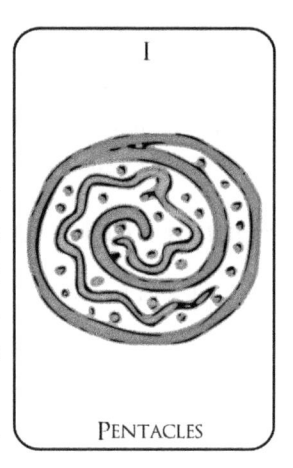

Reversed: A watered down version of the above. There is potential for a new opportunity in business but the questioner will have to push for it as it won't fall into their lap. There may be a money windfall but it's not likely to be much.

Two of Pentacles

Upright: A balancing act, a tightrope walk whilst trying to keep your balance as you may be struggling to cope with all the demands financial or otherwise in your life. Often shows the division of assets and property due to divorce - a house being divided up. It can show very simply a move of house too.

Reversed: Similar to above. There may be a division of property and assets and the need to balance a finances carefully. An anticipated move of house may be beset by delays and problems for now.

Three of Pentacles

Upright: This often shows the purchase of a property or extensions and renovations to an existing property. This is also connected with building a new life on skills learned in the past. It can mean charitable work in society or learning a new skill which will be for the good of others.

Card Meanings

Reversed: A project which is too big or ambitious to handle right now. House renovations may be too big or expensive to carry out satisfactorily. A person who is capable of being more caring and charitable but is being a little selfish.

Four of Pentacles

Upright: This is about holding on to one's assets and money and being reluctant to let go or spend any of it. It is not miserliness but more a fear of losing what one has worked hard to achieve. Possibly too much concern about money and too much emphasis on it. It will be OK, your financial situation is positive.

Reversed: There could be money problems here, perhaps the questioner has been overspending or had a large bill to settle which has depleted their savings. This would mean someone needs to "cut their coat to suit their cloth".

Five of Pentacles

Upright: A card of sadness and loss. It can show where bereavement has already happened but does not predict it! It's amazing how often this shows up when a person has lost a beloved pet also. It can mean grief or a feeling of being shut out from family or friends or a feeling of being shunned.

Reversed: Loneliness and sadness is definitely coming to an end. Although there is still a feeling of loss it is not debilitating. If a pet has been lost, be assured of the arrival of another!

Six of Pentacles

Upright: A card of the family and the pressures sometimes created through family life. The questioner may well be feeling put upon or taken advantage of by others, particularly regarding money. They may need to stop giving out cash to those who are draining them. The questioner should put their own interests first.

Reversed: Similar to above but shows the questioner may be taking a harder line and begin to stop letting people take advantage of them. Family may need to be stood up to.

Seven of Pentacles

Upright: There has been or will be a deal of hard work to come, but there will be rewards to show for it. Keep going, keep at it as you have the tenacity to make this situation work. If you are wondering if it's worth the hassle, the answer is yes it is. Financial rewards are also very likely by your own efforts.

Reversed: A great deal of hard work has gone unrecognised. This can show a person overburdened at work and under appreciated. It's simply not worth this amount of effort.

Eight of Pentacles

Upright: Very much about education, this card shows we will soon be undertaking a course of learning or even qualifications either under our own steam or through work. Occasionally it can indicate learning achieved though life's lessons rather than formal education. Expect to grow in knowledge.

Reversed: There may be problems at work. A person may be under appreciated or underestimated and therefore not being developed professionally. A lack of training but being expected to perform well anyway. Likely to be taken advantage of by employers. Lack of progress.

Nine of Pentacles

Upright: Money and success are indicated here. Often it shows a person who is actively building for a successful and comfortable life. Material goods and possessions have the emphasis but this is also a time to reflect on successes already achieved and feel peace and contentment with one's lot.

Reversed: Emphasis on material goods which won't bring the

fulfilment the questioner needs in life. A feeling of failure or discontent with one's lot even if it's not true. The danger of making money more important than other things. Materialism.

Ten of Pentacles

Upright: Achievement and satisfaction at the life you have built for yourself. Happy family life and successful commercial dealings. You may not be wealthy but presently in a sound financial situation. This is also a card which indicates a conservative nature. Caution and logic are prevalent here.

Reversed: Similar to above, success and satisfaction are shown here if perhaps not as financially rewarding. Further hard efforts should bring results. The end of a financial and personal phase just before the beginning of a new.

Page of Pentacles

Upright: A steady and thoughtful young person or child. This character is a hard worker and likely to achieve good results educationally or at work through dint of hard work. Possibly travel in connection with work. Advice is to remain cautious where finances are concerned and started saving for a rainy day.

Reversed: This reverses the above. A young person who has not worked hard and probably failed exams due to negligence. This can also point to immaturity where finances are concerned. A person is likely to squander money or have an entitled attitude.

Knight of Pentacles

Upright: This is a young or youthful person who is steady and good with money. A reliable and trustworthy partner, perhaps lacking in imagination but whose heart is in the right place. Travel is well starred as is a new business venture. The Knight would make an excellent business partner.

Reversed: A spendthrift who has run up debts. This is a person with an irresponsible attitude towards finances. A bad business venture or poor investment could lead to financial loss.

Queen of Pentacles

Upright: Usually represents a woman who is money minded and concerned with the material aspects of life. She is usually sensible with money but a negative aspect would be a gold digger who is dominated by all that money can buy. She (or he) might be a subject of envy as they appear to have it all.

Reversed: A tough and materialist woman (or man) who is driven by the desire for money and will always win in a fight over finances. A bitter divorce where money is an issue which seemingly cannot be resolved.

King of Pentacles

Upright: A man (or woman) who is in charge of finances - often at the top of a company. They understand the important of good finance but can indicate a stolid or dull character whose primary concern is material things. A good negotiator in business and a reliable family man if a little unemotional.

Reversed: A miser or selfish person. He (or she) is not to be trusted especially where finance is concerned. He might believe himself to be a hard headed business man but is usually a loser in the long run. Relationships ruined by the love of money.

Swords

Ace of Swords

Upright: A new beginning or cycle in one's life. A positive and strong start, such as a new business, new job or a passionate love affair. Whatever is coming to you will do so suddenly and you will be unable to miss the opportunity presented. Occasionally shows where an operation or procedure is needed.

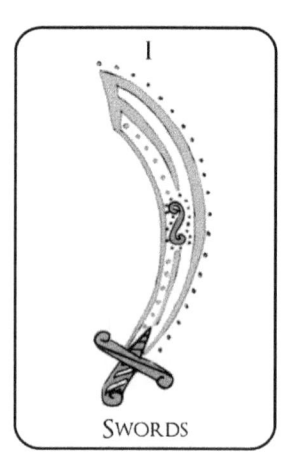

Reversed: Either the above is a watered down version and not quite so absorbing or strong an event but still a new cycle or romance. Or this can be a warning of a poor business decision or even treachery by others.

Two of Swords

Upright: A sense of indecision hangs over this card, it's as though you can't see a clear way forward. There are two paths to choose from and the outcome will be very important. There is a suspension in all matters and delays generally. Expect things to remain as they are for the time being.

Reversed: The indecision will be here for a while, the advice is not to be incapacitated by doubt. Things will sort themselves out soon and the questioner should be able to move forward with confidence.

Three of Swords

Upright: This usually means the end of a relationship or even could relate to the end of a job. In any case expect an ending which may be difficult to deal with at the time. Sadly this card comes with heartache and loss - however, the ground is cleared for new beginnings to come.

Reversed: Sadness and loss are passing quickly now. It is possible this relates to a relationship already ended. It was for the best and recovery is on the way. Sometimes points to when a small medical procedure is needed.

Four of Swords

Upright: This card means recovery - either from physical or even mental illness. If you've been feeling depressed or unwell, be assured recovery is on the way. The other meaning is that you need to take a break from a stressful situation and take time to find balance in your life.

Reversed: Recovery from illness or depression is not yet there. There are still problems to overcome health wise. This can show a person who is unwilling to take positive steps to help their recovery but prefer to wallow in it for sympathy.

Five of Swords

Upright: This is an unpleasant card as it shows conflict. There might be actual quarrels or even violence in some cases. Occasionally this can mean inner conflict where a person is burying their anger and feeling resentful. There may be jealousy or spiteful people around you looking for trouble.

Reversed: As above but the problems are likely to be passing quickly. The quarrels or even violence may already have happened as everyone picks up the pieces. Better times ahead.

Six of Swords

Upright: This card is one of journeys. Either a gradual journeying away from choppy waters into calmer territory or literally travel over water. This is often connected with physical travel and is a positive card as whether literal or figurative, the journey will be positive and most beneficial.

Reversed: Journeys or travel will be delayed and beset by

problems. If this is a metaphorical journey of an emotional nature then this too will be delayed or incomplete. There are still problems which need to be identified and sorted out.

Seven of Swords

Upright: A need to escape mounting problems is indicated here. However, this card can mean a person looking to take the easy way out of things and not facing up to them. They may score an own goal by taking shortcuts or harming others by ill thought-out actions. Theft or a rip off are also shown here.

Reversed: Much the same as above. One should be aware of theft or trickery which is around them now. It does show an enlightenment coming for the questioner regarding their own behaviour or attitude. This should lead to making better choices going forward.

Eight of Swords

Upright: You may feel utterly trapped and unable to change a situation, but the message is that you can, you just need to be bold and take the first step. The chains of enslavement can easily be broken by you. There is a sense of inertia and negativity, perhaps even self pity with this card.

Reversed: The feelings of being trapped are slowly lifting. There will soon be an opportunity to find a way through present restrictions or problems. The problem has not gone yet but it will.

Nine of Swords

Upright: This is a card of desperate worry or anxiety, sleepless nights and a feeling of despair. The only positive point of this card is that the worries are usually greatly exaggerated in the mind of the worrier. This card often means problems with or concerns around one's mother.

Reversed: The terrible anxiety is soon to pass and the questioner should have faith that things will look better soon. The worries of the mind is the biggest hurdle to recovery and often are unfounded.

Ten of Swords

Upright: Being stabbed in the back or some sort of treachery including being gossiped about. This indicates being deceived by another. It can indicate divorce or a job loss, either way there are enforced changes ahead. However, this sad cycle is definitely coming to an end and won't last forever.

Reversed: Only a lesser treachery than the one shown above but still a feeling of having been let down. There may be gossip or slander being passed around about the questioner. This is the end of a difficult cycle and positive new beginnings are beckoning.

Page of Swords

Upright: Watch out for opportunities which will come your way soon. An opportunity is not to be missed often in connection with work. You may need to sign a contract soon. This can show a child or young person with plenty of character and a fearlessness. They may need to be reined in a little.

Reversed: Some spitefulness and childishness behaviour can be expected by the questioner. Be cautious about signing anything official as it may lead to being tricked. Can show poor parenting over a difficult child.

Knight of Swords

Upright: Sudden changes and hasty decisions will need to be made. Expect plenty of swift action if life has been a bit slow up to now. A young person or youthful in attitude, the knight shows a sharp intellect, intelligence and an analytical mind. It's time to analyse a situation in life.

Reversed: An aggressive or belligerent young person who uses bullying to get what he (or she) wants. This is a person who does not care about others and will ride roughshod over feelings. Arguments and difficulties with a selfish and immature person.

Queen of Swords

Upright: A woman of mourning or loss, she is often a widow. She can be a difficult or prickly business woman. Either way, don't expect too much emotion from her, she's a cool customer. She is often a professional woman (or man) who will do a good job but don't expect sympathy.

Reversed: Cold hearted, spiteful and vicious; she is not a kind lady. She may be found in business as a tyrannical boss who is not afraid to make others' lives a misery due to her own feelings of inadequacy and jealousy. She has low self esteem.

King of Swords

Upright: Often represents a man (or woman) whose professional services will soon be needed, whether it's a lawyer, a surgeon or business consultant. He will get the job done and will do it well but, he's unemotional and he can be very difficult to deal with. He might be taciturn or very abrupt.

Reversed: Angry and aggressive, he can be extremely difficult to handle. If the questioner is wondering if they have the right consultant or lawyer on board, this would suggest not. Perhaps a second opinion is needed. This can even indicate a person who is violent.

EXERCISES

The following pages have blank grids designed for you to complete with the information you have already leant from this book. By all means refer back to the various sections to get some pointers, but as far as possible try to draw your own interpretations as these are the ones which will make sense to you and have more meaning rather than trying to remember the classic meanings. It requires some thought and effort but I believe that these exercises are the fastest way for you to learn Tarot.

Please remember there are no rights and no wrongs in Tarot interpretations. More importantly than anything else, is the application of the thoughts that drop into your mind as you look for meanings in the cards. Expand your mind and consciousness and don't be afraid to put down what it tells you even if you think it sounds silly. It's all a question of allowing your intuitive ability to speak to you. Push rational thought and logic to the back and let your psychic abilities have a chance to shine.

You can download large versions of all of these worksheets at:

www.emmapsychic.com/downloads

1: Major Arcana Meanings

Please complete the grid with keywords for your own interpretations of the Major Arcana from what you have learnt in the section on the "Fools Journey"

0	The Fool	
1	The Magician	
2	The High Priestess	
3	The Empress	
4	The Emperor	
5	The Hierophant	
6	The Lovers	
7	The Chariot	
8	Strength	
9	The Hermit	

10	Wheel of Fortune	
11	Justice	
12	The Hanged Man	
13	Death	
14	Temperance	
15	The Devil	
16	The Tower	
17	The Star	
18	The Moon	
19	The Sun	
20	Judgement	
21	The World	

2: Major Arcana Meanings - Reversals

Please complete the grid with keywords for your own interpretations of the Major Arcana cards reversed from what you learnt in both the "Reversals" section and from Exercise 1.

0	The Fool	
1	The Magician	
2	The High Priestess	
3	The Empress	
4	The Emperor	
5	The Hierophant	
6	The Lovers	
7	The Chariot	
8	Strength	
9	The Hermit	

10	Wheel of Fortune	
11	Justice	
12	The Hanged Man	
13	Death	
14	Temperance	
15	The Devil	
16	The Tower	
17	The Star	
18	The Moon	
19	The Sun	
20	Judgement	
21	The World	

3: Minor Arcana – Numbers and Suits

Please complete the grid with keywords for your own interpretations of the Minor Arcana. Remember to combine the numbers' attributes with those of the suits. See sections on the "Meanings of the Numbers" and "Meanings of the Cards".

	Wands	Cups	Pentacles	Swords
Ace				
Two				
Three				
Four				
Five				
Six				

Seven				
Eight				
Nine				
Ten				
Page				
Knight				
Queen				
King				

4: Minor Arcana - Numbers and Suits - Reversals

Please complete the grid with keywords for your own interpretations of the Minor Arcana reversed from what you have learnt in reading the 'reversals' sections of the card descriptions and from your answers in Exercise 3. There is a quick Card Reference Guide at the end.

	Wands	Cups	Pentacles	Swords
Ace				
Two				
Three				
Four				
Five				
Six				

Seven				
Eight				
Nine				
Ten				
Page				
Knight				
Queen				
King				

5: Court Cards - Elements and Suits

Please complete the grid with keywords for your own interpretations of Court Cards by combining the elements' attributes with those of the suits. See sections in "Meanings of the Cards".

For example, the King of Wands combines two Fire elements, whereas the Queen of Swords combines Air with Water. The suit element is always dominant.

Fire	Wands	King	Temperamental, Active, Enthusiastic
Water	Cups	Queen	Emotional, Intuitive, Expressive
Earth	Pentacles	Page	Pragmatic, Grounded, Rational
Air	Swords	Knight	Intellect, Logical, Thinking

	King	Queen	Knight	Page
Wands				
Cups				
Pentacles				
Swords				

6: Court Cards - Elements and Suits - Reversals

Please complete the grid with keywords for your own interpretations of the Court Cards reversed from what you have learnt in reading the 'reversals' sections of the card descriptions and from your answers in Exercise 5.

For example, the King of Wands combines two Fire elements, whereas the Queen of Swords combines Water with Air. The suit sign is always dominant.

Fire	Wands	King	Temperamental, Belligerent, Dominant, Apathy, Unreliable
Water	Cups	Queen	Emotional, Unrealistic, Depressive, Needy, Uncaring
Earth	Pentacles	Page	Unemotional, Unimaginative, Avaricious, Miser, Dull
Air	Swords	Knight	Unfeeling, Dismissive, Cruel, Vicious, Argumentative, Sly

Suit	King	Queen	Knight	Page
Wands				
Cups				
Pentacles				
Swords				

Card Reference Guide

Major Arcana

Card	Upright	Reversed
0 The Fool	Beginnings and journeys, new adventure and expansion.	Rash or foolish behaviour. Infatuation, unable to control emotions.
I (1) The Magician	Creativity, self-reliance, skilfulness and abilities. Taking control. New Business or venture	Out of control. Lacking confidence and self reliance. Moral weakness.
II (2) The High Priestess	Feminine energy, psychic power and spirituality. Trusting instinct.	Denial. Refusing to face truth. Lacking spirituality leading to materialism.
III (3) The Empress	Nurturing, caring, mother, sexuality, conception and pregnancy. The home.	Unwanted pregnancy or infertility. Dissatisfaction with home or lot in life.
IV (4) The Emperor	Authority figure, father, boss such as a boss. Structure and order.	Arrogance, bullying, aggressiveness. Loss of control, frustration and anger.
V (5) The Hierophant	Tradition, conformity, dependability religion and education. Learning.	Unconventional, non-conformist, rebellious. undisciplined Rejecting culture and family.

VI (6) The Lovers	Love, passion, new relationship. Renewed or reunited passion. Familial love.	Unrequited love, failing relationship, lovers parting company. Infatuation.
VII (7) The Chariot	Bumpy journey but a positive outcome. Challenges Problems with vehicles.	No end in sight of difficulties. Others causing problems. Delayed journeys.
VIII (8) Strength	Physical or emotional strength. Returning health after illness. Courageous and brave.	Weakness through adversity or ill health. Depression, cowardice, substance abuse.
IX (9) The Hermit	Contemplation and planning ahead. An important decision. Spiritual guidance.	Loneliness, isolation, obsessive thoughts. Abandoned, rejected and needing help.
X (10) Wheel of Fortune	Life is changing. A stroke of luck. Fluid situation, change. New Opportunity.	Reversal in fortune, unexpected negative event. Temporary setbacks. Challenges.
XI (11) Justice	Legal issues will end positively. Justice fairness, balance. Good business partnerships.	Miscarriage of justice, unfairness. Legal action taken against one. An unfair accusation.
XII (12) The Hanged Man	Life hanging in limbo, can't go back or move forward. Stagnation. Delays, suspension.	Stagnation, a bad situation to be endured a while longer. Patience is needed.
XIII (13) Death	Change. Death of old self and rebirth of the new. Clearing out of life for positive future.	Change, gentle move from old to new. Lethargy, inaction. Bad influences are leaving.

XIV (14) Temperance	Peaceful, harmonious calmer times ahead. Be moderate in all things; be patient, be calm.	Impatience and being too busy to relax. Substance abuse, cleansing is needed.
XV (15) The Devil	Trapped by something or someone. Sexual obsession and toxic relationships. Captivity.	The entrapment is passing quickly. Soon be able to break free. Avoid wicked people.
XVI (16) The Tower	Loss, destruction, disaster. Nasty shock. Illusions shattered, unhappy truth coming.	Long term misery but not sudden disaster. Problems not yet solved. oppression.
XVII (17) The Star	Hope, optimism, good luck. Things will go very well. Recovery from illness. Travel.	Some hope, potential good luck. Talents not being used or dismissed. Pessimism.
XVIII (18) The Moon	Deception, trickery and deceit. Something hidden. Lies, doubt and insincerity. Delays.	Deception and lies around. Try again later. Poor life choices even mental illness.
XIX (19) The Sun	Happiness, joy, good times ahead. Happy marriage and children. A very good omen.	Potential for happiness marriage and/or pregnancy difficulties. Resolvable problems.
XX (20) Judgement	Freedom from control. Retirement, rebirth. Look back at success, make peace internally.	Unsatisfactory endings Guilty feelings. Legal matters unresolved. Selfishness.
XXI (21) The World	Success, all areas will go well. Expansion and travel. Rewards for hard efforts .	Being stuck, unwilling to make positive changes. Cannot accept change. Jealousy.

Minor Arcana

Suits

Suit	Upright	Reversed
Wands	Action, Ideas, Work	Delusion, Egotism, Recklessness
Cups	Love, Emotion, Family	Cold, Unrealistic, Over Emotional
Pentacles	Money, Assets, Materialism	Materialistic, Mean, Greedy
Swords	Ambition, Courage, Power	Anger, Abuse, Conflict

Numbers

Card	Upright	Reversed
Ace 1	Beginnings, Independence, Purpose	False starts, Apathy, Potential Success
Two 2	Relationships, Duality, Choice, Balance,	Difficult Choices, Lack of Confidence, Imbalance
Three 3	Creativity, Social Life, Community, Advancement	Disorganisation, Chaos, Misled by Others
Four 4	Stability, Dissatisfaction, Security, Home	Instability, Insecure, Delays

Five 5	Misery, Conflict, Arguments, Difficulties, Strife	Difficulties Passing, Potential Resolution, Recovery
Six 6	Family, Nurturing, The Past, Sacrifice	Pressure, Being Used, Family Conflict
Seven 7	Mystery, Illusions, Spirituality, Life Choices	Grounded, Lack of Spirituality, Realism
Eight 8	Opportunity, Decisiveness, Strength	Weakness, Defeatism, Indecision
Nine 9	Anticipation, Worry, Stagnation, Hope/Despair	Worries, Anxiety, Stasis, Hope/Despair
Ten 10	Completion, End of a Cycle, Wholeness	Cycle Yet to End, Potential New Start
Page 11	Immaturity, Children, Innocence, Opportunity	Rashness, Foolishness, Problems with Children
Knight 12	Youthfulness, Adventurism, Unreliability, Energy	Thoughtlessness, Unreliability, Hurtful Behaviour
Queen 13	Maturity, Responsibility, Friendships, Nurturing	Immaturity, Selfishness, Spitefulness
King 14	Maturity, Leadership, Drive, Force, Confidence	Immaturity, Arrogance, Weakness